THE TEN POUND
IMMIGRANTS

THE TEN POUND IMMIGRANTS

REG APPLEYARD
with Alison Ray and Allan Segal

Boxtree

First published in Great Britain in 1988 by
Boxtree Limited

Text copyright © 1988 R. T. Appleyard

ISBN 1 85283 220 7

Typeset by York House Typographic Limited
Printed and bound in Great Britain by
Richard Clay Plc, Bungay, Suffolk

for Boxtree Limited
36 Tavistock Street
London WC2E 7PB

Published in association with
Granada Television Limited

Contents

Acknowledgements

We are especially indebted to the four families whose experiences are related in Chapter 8. During interviews over a 22-year period – 1965, 1966 and 1987 – Steve and Pat Throssel, Kathy Dolan, Joe and Mary Aspinall and David and Josie Hall have been extremely helpful and cooperative. Each has provided us with an honest assessment of their decisions to leave England and their experiences in Australia. We are also grateful to many other assisted British migrants who responded to Granada's request published in British and Australian newspapers in 1987 seeking details of their experiences. Only a small number of those who responded could be interviewed, and their experience are conveyed in Chapter 9.

In Australia, Ronald Moore and Richard Borozdin of the University of Western Australia provided us with valuable research assistance. In Britain we are indebted to the assistance provided by Norman Hoffman, former Regional Director (Migration), Australia House, London and to Peter Lindsay and many staff members at Granada Television. Lynne Taylor and Caroline Baird typed the manuscript and we appreciate their efficiency and cheerfulness under pressure at the cruicial final stages.

Although we have made every effort to check the accuracy of information and to interpret it fairly, our assessment has required value judgments. We hope that these are both fair and prudent.

Introduction

British migrants have been the main contributors to Australia's demographic growth. So significant has been their contribution that by 1945 it was estimated that over 90 per cent of the Australian population was British in ethnic origin. Their dominance, facilitated by the establishment of British-type institutions and strong allegiance to the British crown, sometimes gave the impression to outsiders that Australia was little more than an outpost of empire in the south seas.

Australian governments have encouraged British migrants by providing them with assisted passages. Prior to 1945, the numbers of persons who were assisted depended largely upon Australia's economic needs. In periods of depression, the numbers assisted were reduced; in periods of high economic growth, they were increased. The Second World War, however, was in many ways a watershed in Australia's history. The country came close to being invaded by Japanese forces, and this galvanised leaders into adopting policies that would greatly strengthen Australia's capacity to defend itself. Immigration was central to these policies. War-time leaders had argued that a population of at least 25 million (it was then only 7 million) would be required to provide the country with the infrastructure it would need in order to defend itself against future aggressors. To achieve a population of this size by the end of the century would require an immigration intake equal to 1 per cent of the current population every year.

In view of Australia's close political, ethnic and economic ties with the United Kingdom, it was inevitable that high priority would be given to immigrants from that country. The first Minister for Immigration actually expressed the hope that there would be ten British migrants for every non-British one, and successive Ministers, and successive governments, strongly supported immigration policies giving first priority to people from Britain. However, the actual intake of British migrants soon settled at around half the total number of immigrants. The problem of obtaining enough vessels to take the migrants to Australia, the British government's general lack of enthusiasm for the programme, and the availability of potential emigrants from other countries in Europe combined to produce less ambitious targets for the proportion of British migrants.

Recognising that the cost of travel to Australia would prevent many Britons from emigrating there, the Australian and British governments agreed to establish a new Assisted Passage Scheme to subsidise the cost of transporting those young and skilled Britons who were acceptable to Australia as immigrants. Response to the scheme was overwhelming. At one stage in late 1947 over 400,000 persons were registered at Australia House in London for assisted passages. At the time, Britain was suffering severe rationing and shortages; and emigration was a popular means of escape. Indeed, in public opinion polls conducted during the early post-war years, 40 per cent of respondents said they would emigrate if free to do so. While only a fraction of those who replied in the affirmative actually emigrated, over 1 million Britons did go to Australia under the Assisted Passage Scheme between 1947 and 1982. During this period, newspaper, and later television, advertisements constantly urged Britons to write for information about the scheme. Very few Britons would not have been aware of the offer, and probably most of those who failed to respond to it (including those who said they would emigrate if free to do so) wondered what happened to those who did go. Even more important, they almost certainly wondered what would have happened to them if they had emigrated.

This book traces the history of the '£10 passage' scheme, seeks to answer some of the questions asked by millions of Britons who did not emigrate, and gives those who did a chance to compare their experiences with those of others who emigrated. Not everyone who went out to Australia stayed there, and we shall look at the experiences of some who returned to Britain as well as those of migrants who stayed on. The narrative also draws on the findings of academic studies which show general patterns of settlement of Britons in Australia.

The idea for the book grew out of those studies and three television programmes shown between 1965 and 1988 which traced the experiences of three migrant families and a single girl. The first programme, *This England: Take It or Leave It*, screened in 1965, explored and reported the hopes of the emigrants as they prepared to depart for

INTRODUCTION

Australia. The second programme, *This England: The Pommies*, was
filmed in Australia in 1966 and reported the problems and successes of
the same emigrants during their first few months in Australia. The
third programme, *The Ten Pound Tourists*, was filmed in Australia in
1987. Shown by ITV on New Year's Day 1988, and later by the
Australian Channel 9 television network, it reported the experiences of
the migrants over twenty-two years in Australia.

Chapter 1

A Long Tradition

Britain's influence on Australia's life and institutions has lasted a long time and been very pervasive. Colonies established on the far-distant continent and in Tasmania late in the eighteenth and early in the nineteenth century depended for their economic survival on the British treasury and for their defence on Britain's navy. Legal and political systems established in the colonies were those decided and approved by the Colonial Office in London, to which governors were directly responsible. Thus, when the colonies federated into one nation in 1901, the institutions and allegiances they inherited were undeniably British. 'More British than Britain herself' is a refrain running through much of Australia's history.

The British character of Australian society was ensured by the high proportion of immigrants from the mother country, and from Ireland. Unlike the United States, which received waves of immigrants from many parts of Europe, Australia has drawn the overwhelming majority of its immigrants from the British Isles. The convicts transported to Australia were from British prisons and the first pastoral settlers were from British towns and villages. Even the gold rushes of the 1850s, which attracted a relatively large proportion of non-British diggers, failed to undermine the predominantly British character of Australia's colonial population. By 1891, 83 per cent of those living there and born overseas were from England, Wales, Scotland or Ireland.

Despite their dominance in the Australian colonies, the numbers of Britons who settled there during the so-called 'century of migration' (1814–1914) represented only a small proportion of total emigration from the British Isles. To the prospective migrant of that period, the

5

United States and Canada not only offered greater wealth and opportunities, but were also recommended by the fact that they could be reached (and returned from) in several weeks. Australia, tainted by convict origins, was three-months distant on an uncomfortable sailing ship. Although the discovery of gold greatly increased Australia's attractiveness to potential emigrants, the colonies found it necessary during most of the period to offer British migrants financial assistance with their passage costs in order to overcome disadvantages relative to North America. Thus, between 1860 and 1919, 45 per cent of the 1,341,000 British migrants who entered Australia were assisted in some way by Australian governments.

These close demographic links between the two countries were also replicated in both trade and finance. British markets were the destination of most of Australia's commodity exports (especially wheat and wool); and British banks provided most of the capital necessary to exploit Australia's rich resources and to establish government-funded railways, roads and other services. Depression and sustained drought during the last decade of the nineteenth century reduced trade and financial activity but did not affect the close connections which had been firmly established. At Federation, Australia's orientation and its allegiance remained soundly British: a Dominion that proudly played its part in the expansion of empire.

Recovery from drought and depression in Australia during the first decade of the twentieth century also led to a rapid increase in trade, investment and migration. While these developments heartened Australian governments, there was growing concern in Britain about increasing competition in its Empire markets from the United States, Germany and Japan. The British government therefore established a Royal Commission to investigate how the natural resources of Empire countries could best be utilised for the good of the Empire as a whole. In their report, published in 1917, the Commissioners suggested that a common market be formed to exploit the Empire's resources in ways that would keep competitors at bay. Under their plan, the motherland would provide capital and manufactured goods to the Dominions, which, in turn, would provide primary commodities under long-term preferential trade agreements. Britain would also provide the Dominions with the migrants they needed to bring their virgin agricultural land into production.

With the strong support of Dominion prime ministers, the British government then legislated to establish an Empire self-sufficiency scheme under which migration, investment and tariff preference would be linked together. Of special significance for Australia was the passing of the Empire Settlement Act, under which the British and Australian governments would subsidise the passage costs of selected migrants. Australia's leaders saw British involvement in the scheme as a major breakthrough. Hitherto, British governments, while supporting Australian initiatives to assist Britons to emigrate, had resolutely refused to help pay their fares.

Leaders in both countries strongly supported the Empire self-sufficiency concept. Winston Churchill stated that with assistance and perseverance it could affect a revolution in the balance of the Empire's population within a century, and L. S. Amery, Chairman of the Oversea Settlement Committee, saw redistribution of population as a way of alleviating all the economic ills produced by the First World War. Australian leaders were equally enthusiastic. Following his expressions of strong support, Prime Minister William Hughes gave the Commonwealth (Federal) government responsibility for the selection and financial assistance of migrants, a role hitherto taken, in each individual state, by the office of the Agent-General. The Hughes government contributed £12 of the normal £40 fare and also offered to make loans of up to £18 a head to the wives, brothers and sisters of assisted migrants. It also became involved in the supervision of 'landing money', a system whereby £40 was collected from nominated migrants and held in trust by the Treasury to cover contingencies associated with resettlement.

Although 212,000 of the 282,000 British migrants who entered Australia between 1921 and 1933 were assisted under the Empire Settlement Act, at no time did the flow reach the peak of 1913 which had been the aim of planners. Reasons for the less-than-impressive achievement of the Empire Settlement Scheme were carefully examined in three post-mortem reports published in 1932, 1934 and 1938. The main reason given was that Britain's declining birthrate had reduced the importance of the historic role of emigration – to protect the standard of living from pressure of population. A disharmony of interests had also developed between Britain and her Dominions: while it might suit Britain to send large numbers of migrants to the Dominions, it did not necessarily suit the Dominions to receive them. In addition, Australia had embarked on its own industrialisation programme after the First World War, a development that ran counter to the spirit of the Empire self-sufficiency concept, under which Britain provided the manufactured goods and the Dominions the raw materials. Industrialisation also meant that the migrants Australia most needed were industrial workers to man her new tariff-protected industries. These changed priorities and the replacement of labour-intensive with capital-intensive techniques of agricultural production produced, after the 1920s, a rapid decline in the demand for agricultural labour and increased migration from the Australian countryside to the cities.

Empire migration was dealt a severe blow by the Depression of the 1930s, a blow from which it never completely recovered. Although migration recommenced in 1934 and lasted until the outbreak of war in 1939, the viability of Empire self-sufficiency had been seriously questioned. In its 1938 Report, the British government's Oversea Settlement Board suggested that Dominion governments 'examine afresh, and with the greatest care, the question whether, if the decline in the [United Kingdom's] population is found to persist, it can be regarded as in the interest of the British Commonwealth as a whole that migration to the Dominions should continue to be encouraged'. The Board also suggested that, as a result of low birthrates in Britain, the Dominions might examine the possibility of supplementing British migrants with settlers from other European countries. Such a suggestion would have been unthinkable twenty years earlier, but in the case of Australia it proved uncannily prophetic.

Migration between the two countries virtually ceased during the Second World War. The prospect of its renewal was discussed occasionally in both countries, especially towards the end of hostilities, but with more enthusiasm in Australia than in Britain. British leaders could see that the reconstruction of war-damaged industrial and private property would require many more workers than were likely to be available, given adverse demographic trends and human losses during the war. Australia had also experienced high military losses, and its population growth had been affected by trends similar to those affecting Britain, but damage to property had been confined to northern towns attacked by Japanese bombers. None the less, it was anticipated that the demand for housing, consumer durables and government services after the war would require more labour than would be available.

Australia's determination to renew immigration had been strengthened by the fact that the country had come close to invasion by Japanese forces. The war had revealed how vulnerable the large, sparsely populated continent was to external attack. Even before the war ended, Australia's political leaders had decided that the top priority in reconstruction would have to be given to increasing the population from 7 million to a size where it would be able to defend the country against future aggressors. Indeed, Prime Minister John Curtin had suggested during the war that a population of between 20 and 30 million would be necessary to meet this objective. Following discussions in Australia during the final years of the war, the Labour government decided to establish a Ministry of Immigration to devise appropriate policies for reaching the population target. Arthur Calwell, the first Minister of Immigration, calculated on the basis of the experience of the United States that a 2 per cent annual increase in population could be achieved without eroding national living standards. If such a rate were sustained, Australia's population would reach 25 million by the end of the twentieth century. Immigration was destined to play a major role in this objective. Adverse demographic trends during most of the twentieth century had reduced Australia's capacity to increase its population by more than 1 per cent a year through natural increase. The remaining 1 per cent would be achieved through net immigration, which in 1946 meant an intake of 70,000 migrants, increasing each year as the total population increased.

Calwell established and ran the new Ministry of Immigration with the same enthusiasm and single-mindedness that characterised his justification of the immigration programme. Until Labour's defeat in 1949, he constantly reminded his countrymen that successful immigration was the key to Australia's survival. 'We must fill this country or we will lose it', he told the House of Representatives, and reiterated this theme time and again during the 1940s. Nor did he speak in generalities. Asian countries, especially Japan, were the potential enemies; and European countries, especially Britain, were the potential demographic saviours. In a press statement just prior to Labour's defeat in 1949, he observed that when the war ended 'we thought the Japanese might easily come again in a quarter of a century. An eighth of the time [three years] has now elapsed . . . . Can any thinking Australian have confidence that he and his children will not have to face another attack from Japan?. . . . Those hungry covetous eyes are still looking our way. Australia, to Japan, is still part of its Greater Asia Co-prosperity Scheme.'

Calwell also argued that the improved security of Australia through large-scale immigration would have wider benefits. Early in 1947, he suggested to the British government that it would be in Britain's interests too. In future wars, he said, it would not be practicable for British strength to be moved swiftly from one part of the globe to another. The 'loss of Australia', he argued, would place the Empire in a position of having no bases in the Pacific and Indian Oceans. A strong presence in Australia, achieved through British migration, was a viable alternative. The following year he described Australia as a 'British democracy in the Pacific' whose resources should be developed both for the good of the British Commonwealth of Nations as a whole and as a means of deterring future invasion of Australia by Asian troops.

Although Calwell frequently used this type of argument to suit his immediate purposes, he knew from the outset that the long-term justification for a sustained immigration programme – the 'sound and cogent' reason, as he called it – was economic growth. Pent-up demand for goods and services during the war could not be filled by indigenous labour alone, and, although immigrants would be consumers, they would also be producers of the goods necessary to overcome shortages. Indeed, in September 1949, he acknowledged that the great industrial expansion of Australia since the Second World War could not have been achieved without migrant labour.

Calwell left no doubt that he thought settlers from Britain should be accorded the highest priority. His hope, expressed in November 1946, that there would be ten British migrants for every migrant of other origins became the central plank of Australia's immigration policy, even though the British government had warned that in view of the sluggish growth of population in Britain and the country's problems of reconstruction Australia in future would have to look elsewhere for some of its migrants. By May 1948 Calwell had conceded that immigrants would be 'people of our own British stock *and* Europeans of our choice', and in 1947 (or 1948) he told the journalist David Walker that 'we would like the British *and* Nordic races as first priority' (our emphasis).

This was something of a change from Calwell's preference for British migrants alone, but earlier still he had been very suspicious of immigration, and specifically of immigration from Britain. British migrants, he once wrote, had been a 'prop to British capitalist society', a medium for systematically exploiting Australia's resources. His antipathy had been deepened during bitter conflict with the Australian authorities over the conscription issue during the First World War. In 1918 he had written, 'I hope we don't find Australia after the war being used as a dumping ground for "pommies" and cockney outcasts . . . . We want men who are our equals, not our inferiors.' Calwell had entered the Federal Parliament in 1940 dedicated to a policy of socialism. Stormy conflicts with Prime Minister Curtin kept him out of the first Labour ministry. Although further reflection strengthened his views on the need for immigration in general, it did not at first change his mind about British migrants. Calwell's 'new order' would be expedited by working men from many countries, not just Britain. Nor did he change his well-known views on the need for a 'White Australia'. His preferred solution was to have 20 or 30 million people of white extraction, and not 'continue the narrrow policy of having a population of 7,000,000 people who are 98 per cent British'.

The *raison d'être* of Australia's post-war immigration policy had been announced in Parliament by Acting Prime Minister Forde on 15 November 1944. Based on research begun during the early war years by the Department of the Interior, and culminating in a report published during October 1944, it confirmed that British migrants would have to be supplemented with migrants from other white countries, a development which Prime Minister Curtin had foreshadowed during April that year. On Curtin's death in July 1945, Prime Minister Chifley established a new Ministry of Immigration with Calwell as its head. Early policy statements were strongly supported by the Opposition (especially by Robert Menzies), who argued that such a policy must 'consist first and foremost of the close integration of our ideas of the British Empire and in particular Britain'.

Calwell, in what Moore called a 'stroke of brilliance', then appointed a committee of trade unionists and Labour politicians to examine the availability of migrants from Europe. The Committee recommended, among other things, that Australia should sign migration agreements with a number of European countries. Although the Opposition criticised the Committee's plan as having been largely devised by trade unionists, soon thereafter Calwell announced his '10:1 British' objective. Moore believes that this significant turnabout in Calwell's thinking was partly due to a 'cooling of attitude' towards non-British

11

migration when he heard of the amazing interest being shown by British people in emigrating to Australia. Bureaucratic and public resistance to non-British migration also played a part. The Treasury, for example, was very critical of plans for non-British migration; to save public money and 'avoid possible embarrassment to British migrants', it argued that non-British immigrants should not be subsidised. Thereafter, and especially during the remainder of the 1940s, British migrants received top priority in Australia's programme.

From the outset, however, Calwell knew that non-British Europeans would be required to 'supplement' British migrants if his programme was to succeed. In 1945 he told Parliament of plans for publicity campaigns in both Britain and 'other centres of potential immigration on the European continent'. In November 1947 he informed Parliament that Australia now had three streams of migration: from the United Kingdom, from the United States, and from 'war-torn Europe'. And in September the following year he announced that he favoured a 2:1 ratio of British to foreign migrants.

Why had the British proportion fallen so dramatically from Calwell's preferred 10:1 ratio? Immigrants from the United States (mainly servicemen who had married Australians) were few in number; the main non-British intake had come from 'war-torn Europe', specifically from refugee camps. The availability of over a million refugees for settlement overseas was known to Calwell before he visited Europe in early 1947. However, in signing an agreement with the International Refugee Organisation, he was influenced by the favourable impression he had formed on visiting the camps, of the refugees' potential contribution to Australia's economic and demographic growth; by the fact that the IRO had agreed to provide ships to transport selected refugees to Australia and to allow the Australian government to place them in specific jobs for two years; and by his belief that Australians would not resent but rather welcome refugees who would fill jobs for which local labour could not be found. The 170,000 displaced persons who arrived in Australia between 1948 and and 1952 were mainly responsible for a reduction in the British proportion to 50 per cent.

Despite this, Calwell incessantly reaffirmed his preference for British migrants. On 5 March 1946, he declared that British migration 'is first and foremost in our plans'. In January the following year he acknowledged Australia's interest in displaced persons but assured Britain that no genuine British migrant would be denied a berth to

Australia 'in deference to migrants . . . of any other nationality'. In July 1948 he reiterated Australia's policy of looking 'first to its kinsfolk in the United Kingdom'. For Australia, he declared, 'with its predominant British ancestry, the United Kingdom offered the best source of new citizens'. And in March 1949, in response to complaints that displaced persons were being given priority, he retorted that 'it has always been, and will continue to be Government policy to give first preference at all times to British migrants'.

Even though historical ties had been mainly responsible for the preference he accorded British migrants, Calwell and his advisers also knew that British skilled workers, trained in a system similar to Australia's, would be readily accepted by Australian employers and unions. In an article he contributed to *Imperial Review* in July 1946 Calwell wrote, 'Apart from any natural preference we may have for our own kith and kin, from a realistic viewpoint, we are anxious to obtain the services of first class craftsmen – and where else in the world is the standard of skill higher than in Britain?' In August the following year, in response to criticism from the *Sunday Express* that only unskilled jobs were available to British migrants, Calwell reiterated that any Briton who had served a full apprenticeship in the United Kingdom or was fully qualified as a professional would have no difficulty in obtaining congenial and well-paid employment in Australia. Indeed, one of the hallmarks of post-war British migration to Australia, as will be shown, is the high proportion of skilled workers. Successive governments have thus exploited a resource that is entirely compatible with Australia's skill needs and standards.

Calwell and his advisers recognised that the shortage of houses in Australia, caused by the cessation of construction programmes during the war, would be a major problem in achieving targets of 70,000 migrants or more a year. In his speech to Parliament in 1945 in which he set British 'priorities' he also said that high priority would be given to migrants sponsored by relatives who could provide accommodation. In 1948, he estimated that Australia would need to build 750,000 houses during the next ten years in order to meet local and migrant demand. Calwell was constantly aware of the need to avoid the kind of problems that had been experienced by British migrants who arrived under land-settlement schemes during the inter-war period. These, he said, had 'left a bad taste in both Australian and British mouths for two decades'. The key to success was planning: no 'square pegs in round holes' as in the inter-war years. Those who came under the new programme, he said, would be absorbed on a sound vocational and economic basis.

Calwell's concept of sound planning also included obtaining strong support from the Australian public. State immigration ministers agreed to meet capital expenditure on hostels in which migrants would be temporarily accommodated on arrival. An officer skilled in industrial and trade-union matters was appointed to Australia House in London to handle trade qualification matters, and the trade-union movement announced that it planned to enlist the support of every Australian worker to accept migrants as co-workers and fellow citizens who would work under the same conditions and receive the same rates of pay as themselves. Churches and service organisations also gave unanimous support to the programme. By 1947 it was poised to become an influence of abiding significance in Australia's post-war economic development.

Chapter 2

Euphoria

On his return from Europe in August 1946, Albert Monk, the Australian trade-union leader, confirmed to the government that thousands of Britons had enquired about emigrating to Australia. The magnitude of interest was thereafter measured by changes in the numbers of persons who had registered their intention to emigrate at Australia House, London. In November 1946, Calwell told Parliament that the 63,000 applications received for assisted passages (representing 153,000 people) was only a 'token indication of the flood of applications which could be expected once the schemes come into operation and our publicity to encourage migration is intensified'. The number of persons registered at Australia House increased to 240,000 in May and 400,000 in November 1947, followed by another 100,000 written and counter inquiries during the first four months of 1948. Calwell was delighted. The interest shown by Britons assured the achievement of both his overall target and the targets set for British immigration. In August 1947, while admitting that some displaced persons would be accepted by the Australian government, he said that Australia would prefer British settlers and 'could employ 200,000 tomorrow if they could be landed'.

The magnitude of interest is not difficult to understand. Britain had suffered six years of war, in which factories, homes and ports had been demolished or damaged by sustained bombing. The people had been subjected to severe rationing of fuel, food and clothing; services had been drastically reduced and there was little opportunity to replace essential goods that had been destroyed or had worn out. The Royal Commission on Population (1949) attributed the high level of interest in emigration to a number of other factors: fear of another war in Europe in which the British Isles would be particularly vulnerable, and widespread doubt about Britain's capacity to recover from the economic difficulties caused by war, especially the decline of industrial capacity and loss of overseas assets.

Recovery of industrial production was, however, surprisingly rapid: between 1945 and 1947 reconstruction and the export drive to earn crucial dollars had increased demand for labour in Britain and therefore avoided what many believed would be an economic depression similar in magnitude to the one experienced after the First World War. High export earnings had been achieved partly by reducing local consumption. As a result, 1947–50 were lean austerity years when Britons were forced to accept controls and shortages at least as severe as those they had suffered during the war, when sacrifice was the price for survival. Indeed, severe rationing did not abate until well into the 1950s. In this post-war limbo of rationing, shortages and government controls, some Britons understandably looked beyond the shores of their homeland for a place to settle.

Australia had become a favoured destination for Britons because, under the Empire Settlement Scheme, the cost of travel had been reduced to a few pounds for each adult. Aside from Australia's proven loyalty as a wartime ally, evidence of the country's prospects and achievements had been strikingly manifest to British civilians by the appearance, wealth, friendliness and openness of Australian servicemen who were stationed in Britain during the war, and to British servicemen who fought alongside Australians in the Middle East and other theatres. Then, during the period of severe shortages and rationing after the war, the food-parcel programme gave Britain further evidence of the relative abundance of Australia and also the care and support shown by Australians for their difficulties. During his visit to Australia in 1947, the journalist David Walker was astounded by the magnitude of the food-parcel programme. For example, the Victoria League of Melbourne had been responsible for sending over 2 million food parcels to Britain. 'Food for Britain' neatly packaged in 11-pound parcels, 'was not merely begged for in the street, but preached from pulpits and advertised for in the Press.' Hardly a town visited by Walker did not have some local event in aid of the food-parcel cause. Nor was it simply a 'momentary act of generosity engendered by the blitz or war but something that was continuing for years'.

16

In presenting the restructured Assisted Passage Scheme to Britons, Australian politicians and officials exploited the high regard in which Australia and its opportunities were held. Calwell also emphasised relative conditions in both countries. Though he acknowledged that it would be difficult to persuade Tynesiders, Clydesiders and the people of South Wales to leave their homes, he was confident that 'in the clean air and warm sunshine of my country such people will find a niche'. Emigration, he argued, would alleviate the overcrowding, distress and unemployment which was the fear of Britain's most underprivileged areas. He also appealed to demobilised servicemen, the 'younger ones . . . , who would appreciate the first-rate conditions and emancipated status of the working man in Australia', noting that during 1946 over 5000 British ex-servicemen had already settled in Australia. The previous year he had declared that not the least of his duties as Minister was to assist war-weary Britons who so desire to begin a new life in 'our sunny southern continent'.

The Australian government's publicity network was not organised in a formal manner until the late 1940s. Indeed, Australia House could hardly cope with the unsolicited response for information from British people in all walks of life. Though the content and emphasis of some of its publicity was later to be questioned, during 1947 and 1948 the Australian government insisted that it was confining its information to factual material that did not gloss over the serious housing shortage or suggest that Australia was 'a land with gold in the streets'. In much publicity, however – for example, that circulated among the British Occupation Forces in Europe – the predictable facets were emphasised: sunshine, opportunity and 'pretty, brown-legged Australian girls'.

Many Britons in the late 1940s therefore saw Australia as a sunny, prosperous land where a man could earn higher wages and not be bound in his spending by a network of officially devised restrictions. It was a classless society where a man was paid according to his worth, and his achievements were not dependent on breeding, background and education. Working-class men could rise to positions unattainable in Britain, and, though many potential emigrants knew that they would never reach high positions, they believed that their children would have opportunities to do so. Nor was this Shangri La a foreign land, a place where you had to battle with a different language and foreign ways of doing things. It was a British country, populated by

17

people descended from British migrants, whose loyalty to the motherland in two recent world wars had been proven beyond doubt; a
friendly place where Britons were welcomed as brothers. Was it any
wonder then that tens of thousands of Britons applied for assisted
passages even before the scheme had been officially launched?

Given the high priority accorded immigration from Britain, it is not
surprising that Australia's first post-war migration agreement was
made with the United Kingdom. Indeed, proposals for the continuance
of assisted migration after the war under the terms of the Empire
Settlement Act of 1922 had been discussed at a meeting of British and
Dominion prime ministers in London during May 1944. All prime
ministers readily accepted the British government's proposal for a *free*
passage scheme for British ex-servicemen similar to the one that had
operated after the First World War. But, except for Australia, the
Dominions were non-committal about re-establishing an assisted-
passage scheme for civilians. Australia's readiness to negotiate such a
scheme was a direct result of its determination to launch a large-scale
migration programme dominated by British migrants. Although
Australia's officials and politicians knew that rehabilitation of its own
servicemen would have to be given priority, and that there was a
massive shortage of housing in Australia, they also believed that these
problems could be resolved in addition to carrying out a migration
programme.

Following further discussions between the two countries, the United
Kingdom-Australia Free and Assisted Passage Agreements became
operative on 31 March 1947. The schemes would operate only so long
as conditions favourable to settlement existed in Australia and so long
as each assisted migrant had a reasonable expectation of employment
on arrival. Ex-servicemen were granted free passages paid by the
British government, and selected civilians would pay £10 per adult and
£5 for each child aged 14–18 years. The remaining costs would be
shared by the Australian and British governments. The British government would have the right to refuse support for persons whose
expertise was urgently needed at home; and the Australian government
would select the migrants and provide for their placement and after-
care in Australia.

From the outset, the Australian government was careful not to
embarrass the British government by seeking a large number of
specialists in short supply. On the other hand, given the large number

18

of applicants who had registered for assisted passages, and the limited shipping available to take them to Australia (a constraint that would soon loom large in the programme's operation), the government sought migrants with skills in short supply in Australia. A priority selection schedule was devised which gave top priority to single, highly skilled workers nominated by Australian residents who could provide them with accommodation. Such migrants, in addition to filling key employment vacancies, would require only one shipping berth and, on arrival, would not exacerbate the very difficult housing situation. In his speech to Parliament on 22 November 1946, in which he announced these arrangements, Calwell also made first reference to the use of hostels for migrants: 'establishments no longer required or hostels that were established during wartime'. These too would loom large in the programme's future success. He also assured Parliament that all British migrants would have the same social entitlements as Australians.

The high priority accorded building tradesmen is shown by the fact that, even before the Assisted Passage Agreements were signed, 600 British tradesman had been selected for construction work in Canberra. To ensure a fair distribution of the limited number of skilled British migrants, a system was devised whereby shipping berths were allocated on the basis of each state's demonstrable needs. Priority in selection was given to migrants with needed skills who had been offered jobs by employers prepared to guarantee accommodation. State governments provided initial accommodation for seven days in reception centres, and state organisations – churches, settlers' leagues and the Country Women's Association – provided informal social-welfare services.

Throughout 1943 and 1944 British leaders had expressed strong support for the renewal of assisted migration at the end of hostilities. In May 1943, Viscount Cranborne declared that it was British government policy to encourage emigration; four months later the Parliamentary Under Secretary of State for Colonies said that the government was 'definitely in favour of assisting migration within the Empire'; and in December the Parliamentary Under Secretary of State for Dominion Affairs concluded that emigration should be encouraged. Although Calwell was heartened by these expressions of support – indeed, he quoted them in his 1945 speech to Parliament – he knew that they were based mainly on the British government's wish to maintain the British character of Dominion populations. This was a weak reed on which to lean for achieving a large-scale immigration programme in which 10 out of every 11 immigrants would be British. Of even greater concern were the low rates of population growth in Britain and the anticipated high demand for labour there at the end of the war, likely to make it difficult to ensure a sustained supply of immigrants from Britain.

By December 1946 Calwell knew that the British government was not as enthusiastic as his government in supporting the proposed Assisted Passage Scheme. When called upon to refute a report that the British government was lukewarm about his programme he spoke of its co-operation in despatching the first large party of officially sponsored migrants. Two months later the *Bundaberg News Mail*, a Queensland paper, declared that the Attlee government was 'entirely opposed' to sponsoring the departure of workers from Britain. 'There is too much for them to do here', it declared. In branding the report untrue and mischievous, Calwell released a cable from Attlee which he claimed showed that the British government was determined to stand by the Assisted Passage Agreements. The message was not, however, unequivocal in its support: 'We are anxious to help to the best of our ability in providing the additional manpower which Australia needs. And we hope it will be possible to make such arrangements as well as avoid any conflict of interests arising out of your needs and our own difficult manpower problem.' Thereafter Calwell preferred to quote the more fulsome support of the British High Commissioner in Australia (the Right Hon. E. J. Williams), who said he expected his government to play 'as great a part in the future as in the past in the building of the great Commonwealth of Australia'.

Calwell visited Europe during early 1947 with several objectives in mind, not the least of which was his determination to secure the British government's unequivocal support for the Assisted Passage Scheme. Though his presence and his statements were widely reported in the British press, Calwell made little progress with the Attlee government, struggling politically and preoccupied with finding sufficient vessels to carry export goods to the United States. Providing vessels to take emigrants to Australia at a time when skilled workers were in short supply was not a high priority for the British government. On his return to Australia Calwell was asked by a journalist in New York to comment on a speech made by Winston Churchill the previous day to the Conservative Party Conference. Churchill had acknowledged that some of the 500,000 Britons who had indicated interest in emigrating to

Commonwealth countries needed to go for 'family and other reasons', but he had pleaded for others not to leave the sinking ship: 'Stay and fight it out. If we work together with brains and courage as we did not long ago we can make the country fit for all our people. Don't desert the old land: we cannot spare you. The socialist attempt to conscript labour is only a passing phase. Britain will rise again in all her strength and freedom.'

The reaction of Calwell, a Labour government minister, to the Conservative leader's plea was predictable: Churchill had shown disinterest in both the future of the British Commonwealth and of those Britons living 'under almost starving conditions' who had elected to enjoy a fuller and better life elsewhere. And, although the debate was short, its initiation by the illustrious wartime Prime Minister at a time when Britain was experiencing a severe shortage of skilled labour represented a watershed in post-war British emigration to Australia. Indeed, Calwell later conceded that Churchill's intervention had 'submarined' some of his efforts to obtain an Assisted Passage Scheme that was satisfactory in both terms and numbers to the Australian government.

Although Churchill's intervention reflected the Conservative Party's migration policy (soon to be implemented following the defeat of the Attlee government), it was not the central constraint on the programme's success. Shortage of shipping in which to transport emigrants to Australia played that role. The Second World War had reduced the British Commonwealth's shipping fleet from 21 million to 7.5 million tons and placed passenger shipping in a worse position than it had been at any time. At war's end there was not one regular passenger ship sailing between Britain and Australia. As one Australian immigration official noted, regular passenger ships were now either troop auxiliary cruisers or were at the bottom of the sea. This situation led the Australian government to allow the Ministry of Immigration to maintain wartime regulations concerning the use of shipping. Priority in the allocation of berths would be given to persons who were required to travel in the national interest, Australians who had been unavoidably detained in Britain during the war, and Australian wives who had married abroad during the war.

Realising the seriousness of the shipping situation, Calwell established an interdepartmental committee to report on the feasibility of building ships in Australia. The Committee concluded that, because of

Australia's limited industrial capacity, it would take probably ten years to build the passenger ships necessary to transport the planned numbers of immigrants from Great Britain. At the end of 1946, Calwell told Parliament that shortage of shipping was the crux of the problem in bringing migration plans to fruition. Although everything possible was being done to obtain shipping, the main success reported by Calwell at the end of 1946 had not required civilian shipping: over 5000 British sailors, airmen and soldiers who had been stationed in the Pacific elected to take their discharges in Australia.

The situation had not improved by January 1947. While Attlee had indicated his willingness to try to find more shipping space, the British High Commissioner to Australia said that all available British ships were transporting troops for Palestine, Greece, Burma and Malaya; that peace had not yet been made with Italy, and ships were needed to transport large amounts of food to Germany and to send dollar-earning exports to the United States and Canada. The shipping situation, declared one state minister, practically controlled the immigration scheme.

The strength of Calwell's commitment to British migration is shown by his assurance to state ministers that, even though he was investigating the possibility of persuading the United States government to shift displaced persons to Australia in American ships, 'all visas issued to people in Europe were stamped "not valid for travel to the United Kingdom", so that any alien desiring to leave Europe for Australia would have to travel on non-British ships from continental ports'. Even Polish people who had obtained refuge in Britain during the war and were not prepared to return home at war's end could not obtain the concessions planned for British migrants. 'Our view,' said the Victorian Minister for Immigration, 'is that the greatest difficulties would arise if these migrants were brought out whilst there are so many British people willing and anxious to migrate to this country.'

Despite his commitment to British migration, Calwell was not prepared to allow British migrants to travel in uncomfortable conditions. He was less concerned about non-British migrants. When a group of aliens travelled to Australia in 'troopship conditions', sleeping between decks in hammocks, he declared that these conditions were unsuitable for British migrants. Furthermore, 'no shipping berth considered suitable for a British passenger would be given to an alien'.

Though confident in February 1947 that the British government was doing everything possible to alleviate the problem, by June he had clearly lost patience with the rate of progress and had decided to go to both Britain and the United States primarily to obtain more ships to bring migrants to Australia.

> Hundreds of thousands of very desirable migrants are waiting in the United Kingdom, Europe and the United States to come to Australia. If we could find ships, Australia's industrial manpower problem could be solved tomorrow . . . . I will confer with British Ministers and government representatives and heads of shipping lines and examine the possibility of chartering additional ships . . . . I will see the Admiralty about getting an aircraft carrier and converting wartime troop carriers for use as migrant ships.

Every shipping possibility was explored by the determined Minister. On his return to Australia he reported his achievements, and near-achievements, to Parliament. He had persuaded the British government to make available the *Asturias*, with a passenger capacity of 1750 persons in cabin berths and troop-deck accommodation, for two voyages. She would terminate at Fremantle, where migrants would disembark and travel by rail to the eastern states. The troop-deck accommodation would be filled by Polish servicemen and Maltese full-fare passengers; all other accommodation would be allotted to British migrants.

Although the British Admiralty had agreed to make the aircraft carrier *Victorious* available to carry 1000 migrants and make four trips per year, the plan was dropped when the Royal Australian Navy found it could not provide the personnel necessary to man the ship. Calwell reopened negotiations with the British government and Cunard for chartering the *Aquitania*, a vessel well known in Australian waters during the war as a carrier of Australian troops to the Middle East. However, the ship, very different from the pre-war luxury liner, could provide only a minimum standard of comfort, and there were other difficulties. A major problem was that she could not terminate at Fremantle, because the town did not have the facilities to accommodate 2000 migrants four times each year. The *Aquitania* therefore

THE TEN POUND IMMIGRANTS

never entered the migrant service. One ship that did was the Orient liner *Ormonde*, which was converted from troopship duties to austerity travel, and started bringing 1100 British migrants per voyage to Australia. At the same time the *Ranchi* and *Chitral* were undergoing conversion from troop-carriers, and attempts were being made to obtain the *Strathnaver* and *Otranto*.

The Australian government's long-term commitment to the migration programme was confirmed by Calwell's announcement that he was investigating the possibility of constructing special migrant ships in Australia and in Britain. Nor had the question of transporting migrants by air been overlooked. Ten DC4 aircraft in regular service could, he argued, carry 10,000 passengers in twelve months. Indeed, his Advisory Council later carefully examined a plan to fly British migrants to a specially constructed camp in north-east Africa from where they would board vessels plying directly across the Indian Ocean to Fremantle. The shorter sea passage would greatly increase the number of voyages that could be completed each year.

The arrangements made by Calwell brought 25,000 free and assisted migrants to Australia in 1948. In his determination to secure transport for as many British settlers as possible, Calwell had snapped up everything that came to hand, from a brand new liner to a burnt-out hulk. As a result, the flow of British migrants to Australia was twenty-five times greater than it had been a year before, an achievement that exceeded his most optimistic expectations. Nor did the priority accorded British migrants falter. In July 1948 he announced that, if President Truman agreed with his request to provide enough American vessels to bring 200,000 displaced persons to Australia, it would mean that 'no berth for a British migrant would be lost'.

By October that year, Calwell was able to announce that the problem of transport had been 'considerably overcome by unremitting negotiation with the United Kingdom authorities'. And by March the following year a number of all-migrant vessels, plus 13 with some berths available for migrants, were steaming between Britain and Australia. Ship-owners had guaranteed berths for 400,000 British migrants during the next five years. The ships had not been obtained easily, he wrote just prior to his government's defeat, but 'persistence convinced the British authorities that Australia was in deadly earnest with its immigration programme'.

24

Successful though the shipping campaign had been, Calwell saw it as mainly a logistic problem. The larger, more difficult problem was to convince British leaders that large-scale emigration to Australia was in Britain's own interests. Thus, any leader who supported his migration plans was quoted with approval: for example, Lord Montgomery, who said that Britain had 18 million more people than it could feed; and Lord Casey, who backed large-scale transfer of manpower and industry from Britain to Australia. As early as 1945 Calwell had argued that manufacturers in Britain should seriously consider moving their complete operations to Australia, bringing 'not only plant and markets but personnel and families as well'. In his Foreword to Dudley Barker's book *People for the Commonwealth*, he supported the emigration of several million Britons to the Dominions during the next few years, and in April 1947 he argued that the population of Britain should be about 30 million and that the remaining millions should be distributed among Commonwealth countries.

Prior to Prime Minister Chifley's visit to London in 1948, Calwell announced that Chifley would continue the discussions initiated by Calwell in 1947 concerning the redistribution of Commonwealth populations. Chifley hoped to raise the matter with Prime Minister Attlee, the Minister for Commonwealth Affairs, Noel Baker, and the Foreign Secretary, Ernest Bevin. Recent events, argued Calwell, had underlined the urgency of large-scale dispersal of Commonwealth resources; and support was growing steadily in the British Cabinet, Parliament and among the great body of British people. Britain, he wrote, had 'millions more than she could support from her own food growing resources . . . the planned transfer from Britain to Australia of communities and their associated industries would merely represent a commonsense solution to the problem'.

While there is no doubt that Calwell articulated more sharply and enthusiastically than his colleagues the mass-migration concept, it was generally agreed by the Australian government that dispersal of Britain's population and industrial resources would have benefits for both countries. Such plans, however, were very long-term. Chifley's purpose in visiting London was to discuss with British leaders how Australia and New Zealand could help Britain earn more dollars in order to purchase the capital equipment necessary for reconstruction. Calwell's grand scheme for redistributing population and industrial resources were not activated and, indeed, could not be. In the short term, agreement on ways to increase dollar earnings were more relevant; and, as reconstruction caused a serious shortage of labour, thoughts of emigration on the scale necessary to reduce Britain's population to 30 million receded into the mists of unreality whence they had come.

Chapter 3

Australian Policy

The defeat of Australia's Labour government late in 1949 ushered in a near-quarter century of Liberal rule, much of it under the leadership of Robert Menzies. During his prime ministership the Australian government remained dedicated to large-scale immigration and continued to accord high priority to British migrants. Menzies was an incurable Anglophile, whose support for retaining and strengthening Commonwealth (Empire) ties is shown both by his pronouncements to that effect and by his choice of ministers for the immigration portfolio. His first Minister for Immigration was Harold Holt, who in due course succeeded him as Prime Minister. One of Holt's first decisions was to implement annual Citizenship Conventions at which hundreds of people from all walks of Australian life gathered in Canberra to hear and discuss addresses given by distinguished Australians on the importance of immigration. Of especial importance at these conventions were the contributions of representatives of the Good Neighbour Council, a government-funded organisation dedicated to helping newcomers 'assimilate' to the Australian way of life.

The Citizenship Convention was the platform from which Ministers for Immigration announced and defended their policies for the ensuing year. Defence, however, was hardly necessary, as immigration was one of the few political objectives on which there seemed to be no disagreement. Indeed, in opening the first Citizenship Convention in 1950, Menzies not only acknowledged bipartisan support for immigration but declared that the efforts of his Labour adversaries, Ben Chifley and Arthur Calwell, 'deserve the deep gratitude and warm praise of every Australian'. For a decade thereafter, Labour shadow ministers used the Convention podium merely to support the immigration programme; only occasionally did they quibble on such matters as employment conditions and housing shortages in Australia.

At the first convention, Holt also left no doubt concerning the importance he placed on immigration from Britain. In announcing plans for 200,000 migrants from all sources in the ensuing year, he declared that half would come from Britain, 'in order to retain, as much as possible, the fundamental composition of the population . . . . This is a British community, and we want to keep it a British community living under British standards and by the methods and ideals of British Parliamentary democracy.' Holt did not share the fears of some Australians that the already large number of 'displaced person' migrants would weaken the country's British character, but, in order to maintain the position, it would be necessary to 'keep a proper balance of migrants so that the British element will predominate and that our British institutions will persist'.

Of the 100,000 British migrants expected to enter Australia in 1950, 70,000 would be assisted. This total would be far greater than that achieved in any previous post-war year, when only Britons who had been nominated by Australian families and employers were accepted. This restriction, imposed mainly so as not to exacerbate the housing shortage in Australia, had excluded from selection hundreds of thousands of Britons who could not find a relative or employer in Australia willing and able to nominate them and provide accommodation. Seeing signs of a fall in the number of potential personally nominated immigrants, Holt announced the introduction of the Commonwealth Nomination Scheme, under which the Commonwealth government would nominate selected migrants and place them on arrival in hostels, or in the reception centres that had been used to house displaced persons on their arrival. The objectives of the new scheme, announced Holt, were first to ensure that British migrants who otherwise would not have an opportunity under the personal nomination system could emigrate to Australia, and, second, to acquire the labour necessary for essential industries.

Only 180,000 migrants (80,000 from Britain) actually reached Australia in 1950, because, Holt explained at the 1951 Citizenship Convention, the Korean War had caused diversion of some ships used for migrants. However, Holt devoted less attention to this shortfall than to 'fears' which had been persistently expressed in Australia during 1950 concerning the demographic and, hence, the ethnic impact of large numbers of displaced persons. These fears, declared Holt, were groundless. So long as half the total number of immigrants were British, 'we can go on indefinitely . . . without substantially altering the overwhelming British preponderance in our population'. Indeed, he quoted statistics showing that 97 per cent of Australia's population was of British origin. He also took to task critics who argued that immigration was inflationary. If this could be proven, and he did not acknowledge that it could, he wanted to know where the cuts would be made. Not in assistance to migrants, he suggested; nor would anyone seriously suggest that the government reduce the numbers of British migrants on assisted passages. It was difficult enough to get British migrants, he said, and, having initiated a flow which was the envy of other Dominions, it would be foolish to abandon that advantage.

Holt announced a migration target of 180,000 at the 1951 Convention. And, while he expected that 80,000 of these would be British, and that the newly-established Commonwealth Nomination Scheme would play an important role in ensuring this, he also told delegates that the government respected the British government's concern that Australia should not select an unduly large number of skilled workers. As a signatory of the Assisted Passage Scheme, the British government frequently asked Australia House to resist selecting workers with skills desperately needed in Britain. For example, when Britain was short of coal in 1950, 'the government told us politely but firmly that it did not wish us to offer inducements to coal miners . . . and we were asked to give assurance that if any miners desire to come [to Australia] we shall remind them that their government wishes them to remain where they are'.

By 1951, the 50 per cent British proportion had been firmly established. Shipping remained a constraint, as did the British government's wish that Australia should avoid selecting workers considered crucial for economic recovery. Thereafter, however, until his replacement as Minister for Immigration in 1956, Holt never failed to emphasise the central importance that his government placed on maintaining that proportion, and the crucial role that the Assisted Passage Scheme played in its achievement. For example, he was quite self-congratulatory when announcing in 1952 that, although the target for 1951 (180,000) had not been reached (actual total 133,000), mainly owing to

29

the drying-up of the pool of displaced persons and to a minor economic recession in Australia, the British proportion achieved was 55 per cent. True, it had been costly to maintain: passage costs of assisted British migrants were on average £120 a head, whereas the cost of bringing a migrant from the Netherlands, with which Australia had recently signed an assisted-passage agreement, was only £37 10s. And, while the Treasury was not happy about the higher cost for British migrants, he justified it by reaffirming that 'we all want British migration of course, and this is part of the price we have to pay for it'.

Holt was also a vigorous defender of the migration programme in general. When, during the 1952 recession in Australia, questions were asked about the need for migration, he reminded Australians that the country was still highly vulnerable to attack and that high rates of economic growth required a sustained intake of migrants. The defence issue also figured prominently in Holt's last two Conventions (1955 and 1956), not only in relation to Australia's vulnerability, but also with regard to Britain's interests. In a speech reminiscent of those made by Calwell in the 1940s, he asked whether in this age of potential atomic destruction the Commonwealth could afford to have so much of its strength, measured in terms of British population and industry, locked into the tiny and vulnerable area of the United Kingdom. He questioned, as had Calwell, whether British political leaders had adequately weighed the significance of Australia's rapid economic growth to their own strategic interests in south-east Asia. Leslie Haylen, Labour's immigration spokesman, readily developed the same theme by declaring that it was indeed horrible to contemplate what could happen in an atomic war to the 'millions of our fellow Britishers in that tight little island'. Even though the Churchill-inspired view about deserting the sinking ship was still widely held in Britain, Australian leaders tried to show Britain that by supporting emigration to Australia they were strengthening rather than weakening the Commonwealth.

Although Holt raised the defence issue again in 1956, when he argued that communist activities in south-east Asia would affect Australia's security, his speeches at that Convention were devoted mainly to reaffirming the central importance of British migration. When the Displaced Persons Scheme ended in 1953, Australia had signed bilateral assisted-migration agreements with a number of northern European countries so as to maintain the total migrant intake at target levels. And, while high rates of economic growth during the

1950s posed no employment problems for migrants, the presence of large numbers of non-Britons had led some critics, especially in Victoria, to ask why the British proportion could not be higher. Holt lost no time in taking the fight into the enemy's camp. Such criticism, he said, was ill-informed. From the outset he had insisted that British migration receive top priority. A large proportion of Britons who had come to Australia since the Second World War had been assisted. Indeed, wrote Holt, 'Emigrate to Australia for £10' is the theme of Australia's migration drive in Britain. So long as Britons fulfilled normal health and character requirements, they would be accepted by the government, subject only to the limitations imposed by the availability of shipping berths and accommodation. The Australian government had recently joined with the British government to purchase a migrant vessel (the *New Australia*) for the sole purpose of bringing British migrants to Australia, and it was likely that foreign vessels would be chartered to keep pace with the demand. 'No limit will be placed on the number of British people who will be given assisted passages. I stress that', said Holt. 'When British people complain that they cannot come here, what they are saying, in substance, is that they cannot find sponsors here or that they do not qualify under the Commonwealth nomination scheme.' Holt's views on British migration were warmly supported by delegates at the 1956 Citizenship Convention, where it was resolved that, despite the high cost of bringing British migrants, there should be no reduction in their privileges. This, it was argued, would ensure that there was no decline in the ratio of British migrants to those from other countries.

Although Harold Holt had been true to his policy of according the highest priority to British migrants, in terms both of generosity of assistance and of proportion of total intake, the sustained intake of non-Britons in almost equal numbers posed a number of issues which successive ministers would be obliged to address. Holt, however, tended to be rather condescending about the contributions made by non-Britons and seemed not to perceive the magnitude of the problems that their presence had raised and would continue to raise in the future. In a pamphlet published in 1952, he emphasised the importance of British migration in keeping Australia as a 'firm British bastion of the Pacific', and merely acknowledged that non-British migrants were also bringing their varied and colourful culture, their traditional arts and crafts, their music, dancing and songs, 'things that will mature our

31

culture'. His tune was still the same in 1956: Australians were proud of their British origins and way of life, but also 'tremendously gratified by the valuable contribution made by migrants from other countries'.

Non-British migrants arriving under bilateral agreements had not been accorded the same assistance with their passage costs as had British migrants. And many displaced persons who had travelled to Australia in inferior vessels provided by the International Refugee Organisation were initially placed in spartan hostel accommodation. Typically unable to speak English, they generally filled unskilled jobs and had only limited prospects of improving their skills. By the mid-1950s, their 'assimilation' had become an important political issue, and so an increasing proportion of Citizenship Convention debate, and newspaper comment, was devoted to ways of resolving their difficulties, especially those relating to language.

Although Holt acknowledged that many non-British migrants were experiencing difficulties, and that his Department was assisting them wherever possible, he appears to have been much more concerned about emerging problems associated with maintaining the British proportion. The Commonwealth Nomination Scheme had been implemented in 1952 to tap the large reservoir of British migrants who could not find a sponsor in Australia. As the nominees had to be accommodated in hostels offering only basic comfort and facilities, preference was initially accorded to single persons or married couples without children. When the supply of such persons diminished the government began to sponsor family units. The experiment was not entirely successful. In 1953 Holt admitted that, while the hostel system 'worked very well' for non-British migrants, it did 'not appear to suit the British temperament and it is an experiment that we are not anxious to expand or to continue indefinitely'. As 1953 was a year of recession in Australia and the immigration target was reduced to 80,000, Holt took the opportunity to suspend the Commonwealth Nomination Scheme. Though rapid economic recovery led the government to increase the intake to 115,000 in 1954–5, by then the 'market' had begun to move in the seller's favour and it was becoming more difficult to secure large numbers of British migrants; emigration was less popular than it had been during early post-war years, when the government was dealing 'literally with mass migration'. Australia's image had also been tarnished a little by economic recession, and it was clear that more effort would be needed to obtain the required numbers of migrants with appropriate skills.

Athol Townley's two years as Minister for Immigration (1957 and 1958) therefore saw the introduction of several schemes offering incentives to potential British migrants. At the 1957 Citizenship Convention he said that Commonwealth-nominated British families, unlike many non-British assisted families before then, would be accommodated together in hostels: the husband would not be housed in single men's quarters and his dependants in holding centres. In announcing his 'Bring out a Briton' scheme, designed to encourage Australians to nominate British families, Townley said that Australian state governments would be asked to send officials to country towns, where accommodation problems were less severe than in the cities, armed with details of potential British migrants who were anxious to settle in Australia but could not find personal nominators. 'If every town took one British family,' argued Townley, 'it would greatly increase the intake of British migrants and also have a snowballing effect.'

Townley also announced his government's decision to introduce long-term, rather than annual, immigration targets, thus confirming commitment to the 'one per cent of population per annum through migration' policy. He also declared that this objective could not be met if Australia confined its intake solely to persons of British stock. 'Stated quite simply,' he declared, 'our main objective is to strengthen the nation's economic and defence capacity through population building', and southern Europeans, who were entering Australia in large numbers to work in the expanding manufacturing sector, would be no less welcome than Britons.

The 1957 Convention was also the first occasion on which the Opposition representative seriously criticised the government's handling of immigration. The point of conflict was the declining British proportion. A young backbencher named Gough Whitlam, also (like Holt) destined to be an Australian Prime Minister, lamented the fact that, when return rates were taken into account, the net British proportion was probably only one third. 'It cannot be a matter of pride to us,' fulminated Whitlam, 'who are descended from people who came originally from the British Isles, that Australia in many ways is not proving as attractive to people from the British Isles as is Britain herself.' Whitlam found it inconceivable that British migrants would not be better off in Australia than at home, and laid the blame on the government's employment, housing and social-security policies. It was a clever ploy for the Opposition spokesman: support the British tradition and blame the declining British proportion on an incompetent government.

Whitlam's criticism was readily taken up by many Convention delegates. By now, the policy of housing British migrant families in hostels (former army camps and converted warehouses) was under attack from all sides. For example, a Mrs Furley of the Liberal Party complained that migrant families in hostels could not afford, after paying their full board, to save the deposit they needed to purchase a house. On the other hand, P. J. Cleary, a Labour politician and a discussion-group chairman, reported that some delegates thought that hostel fees should be increased in order to force migrants to leave hostels. Albert Monk, the trade-union leader, told delegates that the 32 hostels in Australia, with a capacity of 32,000 persons, had only 19,403 residents. The main problem, he said, was not shortage of places but how to encourage the 'hard core' of migrant stayers to leave. These had been identified as persons who refused to avail themselves of the opportunity of finding other accommodation. They were, he said, mainly British migrants. A recent survey had shown that 913 families had lived in hostels for longer than two years. 'Has the time not come', asked Monk, 'when we should adopt a less sympathetic policy towards these people?' A Good Neighbour Council representative from Tasmania also warned against making conditions too easy for British migrants: 'We do not want to induce a number of "inquisitive tourists" to come here, have a look around, and then return to their homeland', he said.

The 1957 Convention was, in many ways, a watershed in post-war British migration to Australia. High return rates (some observers suspected that the rate was as high as 20 per cent), 'hard-core' British hostel-stayers, and the accusation that many Britons had been only 'inquisitive tourists' taking advantage of the £10 passage scheme for a cheap holiday had combined to blemish the previously near-unanimous support for a high proportion of British migrants. The new mood was not unrelated to recognition that non-British migrants, especially the displaced persons, Dutch and Germans, had played significant roles in nation-building. They had proved to be hard workers in jobs avoided by Australians, many had shown skills the equal of Britons, and most had shown loyalty and support for the laws and traditions of their new homeland. The prospect of maintaining a migration programme in which half the intake was comprised of such persons was now more acceptable than it had been in the early post-war years. Thereafter the national debate, in both newspapers and at Citizenship Conventions became more sharply focused on ways to assist the 'assimilation' of the ever-increasing numbers of non-British migrants.

Although opinion polls indicated that Australians preferred migrants from northern rather than southern Europe, dedication to the migration programme in general never waned: 'constancy, steadiness and acceptance of individual risks, must be our watchwords in the great migration programme', declared Prime Minister Menzies in opening the 1958 Convention. His Labour adversary, Dr H. V. Evatt, in developing the theme introduced by Whitlam the previous year, emphasised that the government's economic and social policies had not been appropriate and, in a clear recognition of changing attitudes towards non-British migrants, declared that the 'human and the *cultural* side of building a nation' were just as, if not more, important as the economic side. His strongest criticism, however, was directed, as had been Whitlam's, to the declining proportion of British migrants. It was, he declared, at a 'dangerously low' 30 per cent, when his party believed that it should be 60 per cent. 'What is going to become of Australia if the percentage of British migrants continues to fall?' he asked, answering that the whole composition of the Australian population would alter.

Townley's response was that 30,000 assisted British migrants would arrive by mid-1958. To achieve this, the government had chartered *Fairsea* and *Fairsky*, former carrier escorts which had served both the US Navy and the Royal Navy during the Second World War, and had been converted into passenger ships. They would supplement berths available on commercial vessels. 'I can assure you', he told delegates, 'that the Government will press on with vigour to bring in a maximum number of British people.' The 'Bring out a Briton' scheme, which had been very successful, had already led to a significant increase in British assisted migrants.

The 1958 Convention was probably most notable for the salutary warning delivered by W. D. Borrie, the eminent demographer, who, having carefully assessed the economic and demographic dimensions of British migration, warned that Britain was not an 'inexhaustible reservoir of potential migrants'. Indeed, between 1953 and 1955

Britain was probably a net *immigration* country. If Australia required industrial migrants, argued Borrie, it would have to compete with Britain's own needs. And, from the British point of view, emigration was no longer a clear economic or social gain. Indeed, he told delegates that probably four out of five emigrants from the United Kingdom were being replaced by immigrants from Ireland, Europe and Commonwealth countries.

Though Calwell and others had issued the same warning a decade before, its reiteration by Borrie at the beginning of the 'new era' led even the most dedicated Anglophile to acknowledge that sustained annual migration intakes equal to 1 per cent of the population, only half or one third of which would be British, would inexorably alter the ethnic base of Australia's population. Defenders of the high British proportion put their faith in improving the facilities for British migrants, offering them something 'in exchange for the homes and other things that they were leaving behind', as one delegate put it. Others argued that the publicity network – perhaps headed by a delegation of successful British migrants – should be widened and also that selected migrants should be given an assurance that they would acquire housing in a 'reasonable time'. Increased competition from other countries, especially Canada, meant that Australia would have to offer better prospects to potential emigrants. However, it was Borrie who put the debate into perspective. In the nexus which exists between Australia and Britain – countries with a high degree of cultural and institutional similarity, such as social services and welfare in general – immigration flows are always extremely sensitive. They can therefore be influenced in the short term by relatively small factors arising from publicity and adverse reports. For this reason, he argued, the housing issue *was* important, as was the need to handle publicity in Britain with tact and care and to be thoroughly honest. At the same time, Australians should not be too concerned about the current return rate. It was, he argued, inevitable that in a situation of 'delicate poise' there would be a circular flow of migrants between the two countries. The main concern of policy-makers should be to discover how many returning British migrants had been 'disgruntled' by adverse conditions in Australia.

Although 'delicate poise', housing and the character of publicity would be raised time and again in the ensuing decade, housing was at that time the central practical issue, the kernel of a continued migration scheme. 'You cannot ask a family to leave a home, even a home in a poor street in an English city, and not guarantee to house him in his new country', said Dr Darling, headmaster of a leading Australian private school. In general, the British migrant expects a much better job and much better accommodation than do migrants from other sources. He is also rather less adaptable and less ready to suffer the discomforts and disappointments almost inseparable from the upheaval caused by migration.

A. R. Downer's appointment to the immigration portfolio in 1958 assured Australians that, despite issues raised at the 1958 Convention, pro-British policies would not be eroded. Downer's commitment to the Commonwealth was, like Menzies', complete. To the Millions Club in Sydney in July that year he said that, in order to develop Australia as a British country ('reinforced by settlers from Western Europe'), he intended increasing the flow of British migrants by all practicable means. And, while 'valuing highly the presence of our New Australian settlers', Australia must not allow its basic British characteristics to be too diluted or submerged. Migration policy would therefore be formulated on the basis of a high British content. He gave his personal assurance that every practicable, possible means within the limitations of Australia's economy would be undertaken to increase the flow of British people to Australia.

The 1959 Convention exuded Downer's views and optimism. The Governor-General, Sir William Slim, in opening the Convention, hoped for a sustained high proportion of British migrants if only because most Australians were of British stock and that Britain had contributed most to the world in the understanding and practice of ordered freedom. The British High Commissioner, who followed the Governor-General to the podium, reiterated the British government's commitment to the Assisted Passage Scheme, citing views expressed by the British Prime Minister, Harold Macmillan, during his visit to Australia the previous year. And, while the High Commissioner argued that for Britons with imagination and initiative, there was no more attractive and worthwhile place to settle than Australia, he also said that during the last few years Britain had experienced unparalleled prosperity. There was now no lack of jobs and the standard of living had never been so high. As Macmillan himself had told his countrymen, 'you have never had it so good'. The measure of the United Kingdom's sustained commitment to the Assisted Passage Scheme, he said, was that, while it continued to provide financial support (albeit only a small proportion of the total cost), it made no contribution whatever to the costs of Britons leaving for any other Commonwealth country.

Evatt preached on the same text as he and Whitlam had taken at earlier Conventions: as many British migrants as possible should be admitted. And, while this hope should not be seen as reflecting adversely on New Australians, they must see things from a common-sense point of view. 'Australia is British and the migrants who become naturalised owe allegiance to Her Majesty the Queen.' He therefore congratulated Downer for adopting new methods to attract more British migrants. Downer had reported that over 295 'Bring out a Briton' committees had been established in Australia and that the government had opened new offices in regional centres in Britain in order to attract the 'highest percentage of British migrants to total assisted intake for 31 years'.

By 1959, however, largely because of rapidly improving economic conditions in Britain, the number of applicants for assisted passages at Australia House had declined to a point where, in order to maintain the high British proportion of total migration, it was necessary to grant almost any young family or single person an assisted passage, irrespective of skill. At home, Downer took every opportunity to extol the importance of British migration to Australian society: 'Our institutions and way of life are basically British to which we are contributing, in several important and praiseworthy respects, our own idiom. I hope these fundamental characteristics will ever continue.' Nor did he think Australians needed to be convinced about the desirability of maintaining a high percentage of British migrants: the main task was to convince political and commercial leaders in Britain that the ultimate interests of the British Commonwealth would be best served by a deliberate policy of dispersal of the mother country's population to such proven friends as Australia and New Zealand. Shades of Arthur Calwell!

As the 1952-3 economic recession in Australia had led the government to reduce the intake of migrants, so similar policies were invoked during a similar recession of 1960–1. Recovery, however, was rapid, and by 1963 Australia House reported a 'spirited interest' which reached a crescendo in January and February, making it certain that 42,000 assisted British migrants would arrive in Australia during

1962–3. This would be the highest intake for more than a decade, requiring the government to seek every available place on ships and aircraft. Indeed, the 1960s were in many ways a halcyon period for British migration to Australia. Whereas the British (assisted and non-assisted) proportion had been 42 per cent between 1947 and 1951, it rose to 54 per cent during the 1960s. The narrowing of average real income differences between the two countries during the 1960s seemed to encourage Britons to be more calculating in their assessment of the benefits of migration. Whereas in the immediate post-war years short-ages and fears of renewed conflict had created a desire simply to escape, many Britons now apparently calculated carefully all aspects of the migration decision – real income changes, presence of relatives, climate, lifestyle, and so on. By now, also, there were over a million post-war British migrants in Australia, thus increasing the potential for larger numbers of personally nominated migrants.

The 1960s, too, were a period of high economic growth in Australia. In addition to receiving large numbers of British migrants, Australia admitted thousands of migrants from southern Europe, even though none was accorded the same privileges as were Britons. Australia's Nationality and Citizenship Act of 1948 made British citizens eligible for Australian citizenship after only 12 months' residence in Australia; non-Britons had to achieve five years' residence before being eligible. Britons also received better assisted-passage conditions, were provided with hostel accommodation during initial resettlement, could move in and out of Australia on visits with no difficulty, received preferential treatment when seeking to enter the Australian military forces, and could vote in elections without becoming Australian citizens.

These generous conditions, especially the £10 passage, clearly attracted many Britons who were uncommitted to permanent settle-ment in Australia. Under the terms of the Assisted Passage Agree-ments, a migrant was required to stay in Australia for two years or else refund to the Australian government the cost of his/her outward passage. In the more relaxed climate of the 1960s, this condition led many Britons to 'look Australia over' before deciding whether to settle there. The absence of restrictions on their entry to Australia, and the relative ease with which they could obtain assisted passages, has also been identified as a major reason why return rates were so high. Indeed, in 1961 the rate was calculated at about 20 per cent compared with less than 10 per cent for other nationalities.

Borrie, who had already argued in 1958 that migration flows between the two countries would always, given the high degree of cultural and institutional similarity, be in a state of 'delicate poise', now argued that the prime factor explaining the remarkably large intake of British migrants between 1961 and 1967 was the Assisted Passage Scheme. Furthermore, during this decade of Liberal government, one Minister for Immigration after another confirmed the importance of maintaining the British proportion at around 50 per cent. New programmes were implemented, ranging from the appointment of Professional Liaison Officers at Australia House to increase the number of graduates (1963) to a programme which brought to Australia 200 British undergraduates for their summer vacations (1965). In a brief prepared by his department before making a visit to Europe in 1965, the Minister was reminded that British migration had been, was and would remain a cornerstone of Australia's policy; and that the maintenance of the British connection had 'the first interest of government'. The cornerstone was reaffirmed by another Minister in 1970 when he announced that he was 'positively pursuing a vigorous recruitment policy' in Britain to reverse a recent decline in British interest in emigrating to Australia.

If the 1960s were the halcyon era for British migration to Australia, they were also a period of major change in Australian–British relations which led, in due course, to a dramatic reduction in immigration from Britain and also to the dismantling of the Assisted Passage Scheme. Britain's entry into the European Community in 1972 severed many of the special trade arrangements with Australia which had been established and nurtured over much of Australia's brief history. The subsequent removal of longstanding privileges giving Australians near-unimpeded entry into Britain for settlement led, soon thereafter, to reciprocal restrictions by Australia. The 1960s were also the period when mounting pressure within and outside Australia against its well-known 'White Australia' policy led to a relaxation of restrictions on the entry of non-Europeans. There is no doubt that Australia's new policy was influenced greatly by the initiative of the United States in replacing its long-established quota system (which favoured European immigrants) with a system based on America's need for skilled personnel. However, regional issues also played a part. The 'White Australia' policy had created a great deal of ill-will amongst Australia's Asian neighbours, many of whom had recently achieved independence and were no longer beholden to migration policies devised by, or for the benefit of, colonial rulers. Following reports from Australia's diplomats in Asia concerning the negative influence of the 'White Australia' policy on otherwise good relations, and strong lobbying by small university-based groups, the Australian government slightly opened the migration door to non-Europeans. Initially a few thousand highly qualified and distinguished non-Europeans were admitted, but in due course immigration from Asia became a significant stream.

The initial changes to, and ultimate dismantling of, the 'White Australia' policy was also hastened by the increasing importance of Asia as a region of trade for Australia. Britain's entry into the European Community, and the consequent steep decline in trade with Australia, was accompanied, much to Australia's relief, by the emergence of Japan as a major buyer of its minerals and agricultural goods and, in due course, a major supplier of its imported manufactured goods. By the late 1960s, Japan had replaced Britain as Australia's major trading partner. In addition, the rapid economic growth of nearby countries in south-east Asia (the ASEAN group) provided Australian exporters and importers with new opportunities. These developments also had a significant and lasting impact on Australia's immigration policy. Hitherto, its trade was mainly with countries which also provided its immigrants, especially Britain. Now its trade was with countries whose citizens had been excluded as settlers. With the consolidation of new trade patterns, the old migration policy became increasingly difficult to justify.

The long-standing high priority accorded British migrants also came under scrutiny. As already noted, approximately half of Australia's post-war immigrants had been non-British. In early post-war years, Australia's policy concerning their resettlement was rigidly paternalistic and assimilationist. Newcomers were deemed lucky to be in the country and were expected to become incorporated and absorbed into the Australian way of life as soon as possible. However, after the mid-1960s governments supported (perhaps were forced to support) a milder form of 'adaptation' which signalled greater tolerance of cultural differences and diversity of lifestyles. This was a new experience for Australia, which, unlike the United States, had drawn the overwhelming majority of migrants from one country – Britain. By the early 1970s the sheer numbers of non-British migrants posed new political issues which ultimately were resolved by the newcomers' electoral strength. Prior to its defeat by Labour in 1972 after a near-quarter century of office, the Liberal government had been valiantly trying to come to terms with the Asian and non-British migration issues. In responding to Labour's promise that, if elected, it would expand the Assisted Passage Scheme 'for all', including non-Europeans, Immigration Minister Forbes warned Australians that such a policy would cut *assisted* migration from Britain by more than 60 per cent.

The warning was to no avail. The new Prime Minister, Gough Whitlam, who at the 1957 Citizenship Convention had wondered what would become of Australian society if the proportion of British migrants entering the country did not increase, attained office in 1972 partly by recognising that the new ethnic demography of Australia presented the opportunity for gaining the additional seats necessary to govern. The first Minister for Immigration in the Labour government, Al Grassby, set about initiating the major changes in policy that had been forshadowed in the lead-up to the election. By October 1973 he was able to report that 'every relic of past ethnic or racial discrimination' had been abolished from departmental procedures. Henceforth emigrants would be selected for their ability to contribute to Australia's socio-economic development. A new Citizenship Act was based on 'one criteria, one procedure and one allegiance', and all migrants would be accorded equal treatment in terms of citizenship. Thereafter, all migrants to Australia were encouraged to cultivate, not disown, their cultures as a way of retaining their self-esteem and self-identity. This led quickly to the adoption of a new policy of multi-culturalism. Minority groups in Australia, especially Greeks and Italians, who had arrived in large numbers during the 1960s, were now more aware of their political power. The special position that had been enjoyed by British migrants throughout Australia's history therefore came to an end. Every migrant was henceforth to be accorded the same treatment.

In 1973 the world economy was shaken by the oil crisis. A massive increase in energy costs led Australia, and many other countries, into a period of high unemployment and inflation (known as 'stagflation') from which it has never fully emerged. Earlier post-war recessions, in 1952–3 and 1960–1, had been short-lived; governments had reduced immigration targets slightly but restored them the following year. After 1973, however, stagflation and policy changes concerning the sources from which migrants would be drawn combined to create programmes and settlement policies quite unlike those practised between 1945 and 1972. In this period of stagflation, demand for 'economic' migrants understandably declined and new emphasis was placed on 'family reunion', i.e. encouraging Australian residents to nominate close relatives. Annual immigration intakes declined from 170,000 per annum during the early 1970s to 50,000 in the mid-1970s.

The proportion of British migrants also declined; nor did it recover with the return of a Liberal government in 1975. The decline was accompanied by a progressive reduction in the proportion of British *assisted* migrants in the total assisted-migration programme: 1977, 52 per cent; 1978, 45 per cent; 1979, 17 per cent; 1980, 12 per cent; 1981, 20 per cent. The main reason was that after 1978 the government admitted large numbers of assisted refugees from Vietnam, and the new emphasis on family reunion saw large numbers of Vietnamese relatives enter Australia. British 'economic' migrants now had to compete for fewer places with migrants from all sources. And, although British skilled and professional workers had an advantage over workers from other countries, because their apprenticeship and tertiary training was entirely compatible with Australian systems, stagflation reduced the overall demand for migrant labour.

In 1981, following a major review of the Assisted Passage Scheme, the Liberal government decided that under the prevailing economic circumstances assisted passages were no longer needed to attract to Australia the 'desired size and type of intake'. Prolonged economic recession had greatly reduced the demand for economic migrants, the very category that Britons had dominated for so long. Indeed, between 1976 and 1981, the proportion of net migrants from the United Kingdom and Ireland had been only 22 per cent of the total.

The Assisted Passage Scheme had not only brought more immigrants from Britain than from any other country; it had also had enormous influence on the total flow of immigrants from that country. Between 1961–2 and 1971–2 only 10 per cent of immigrants from Britain were not assisted. Many of these persons were professional or business employees who had been appointed to positions in Australian universities, government and commerce or were well-to-do persons who preferred not to utilise the Assisted Passage Scheme.

Chapter 4

The British Response

Australian governments have clearly been more interested than British governments in the success of the Assisted Passage Scheme. At the end of the Second World War, reconstruction of war-damaged property and the need to increase exports, especially to the United States, required more labour than Britain could muster from its own population. As Borrie has shown, the number of immigrants to Britain from continental Europe, Ireland and, after the early 1950s, Commonwealth countries, both developed and developing, all but cancelled out the loss of British emigrants to Australia, Canada and other countries.

For the British government, there was, in fact, little economic or demographic logic in encouraging Britons to emigrate, and even less in financially assisting them to do so under the United Kingdom–Australia Assisted Passage Agreements. Justification for maintaining the agreement with Australia was therefore largely political: to strengthen and maintain the British element in Australia's population. Not only did the Oversea Migration Board consistently put forward political, strategic and economic reasons why the British government should retain the Assisted Passage Agreements with Australia, but the 'Commonwealth ties' argument dominated every debate on post-war migration in the Houses of Commons and Lords during the 1940s and 1950s.

Under these circumstances, it is hardly surprising that British governments progressively reduced their financial contribution to the scheme. From an arrangement of equal sharing at inception, Britain reduced its share in April 1950 to a maximum of £25 per adult. The British contribution was further reduced to a maximum grant of

£500,000 in March 1951 and to £150,000 in 1954. While these cuts were justified by the government on the grounds of 'financial embarrassment', the Oversea Migration Board defended them on the basis that, because the Australian government made up the balance of each cut, not one prospective settler under the scheme had been in any way deterred from taking advantage of it. The Board also argued that Britain had already borne significant costs in training and educating migrants who left under the scheme. Furthermore, by remaining a partner in the scheme, it could influence Australia to take a fair cross-section of the British population. While there is no doubt that Australia was more even-handed than other Commonwealth countries in this regard, assisted British migrants, as will be shown, clearly had above-average 'characteristics' and achievements. Britain's annual contribution of £150,000 continued until 1972, when the government decided to terminate the agreement – again for financial, not political, reasons. Although the Australian government argued strongly against the severance of yet another formal tie between the two countries, no new agreement was signed. The British government's withdrawal was not an overnight decision: it had clearly been influenced by weakening trade and political ties between the two countries, especially after Britain's entry into the European Community.

The British government's declining contribution to the Assisted Passage Scheme was in stark contrast to the sustained interest shown by Britons themselves in emigrating to Australia under the scheme. Not only had the reserve of applicants at Australia House been measured in hundreds of thousands between 1947 and 1952, but the remarkably high level of interest shown by British people in emigrating to *any* country was thought to reflect widespread dissatisfaction with economic and social conditions at home relative to perceived conditions and opportunities in such countries as Australia. To the question 'If you were free to do so, would you go and settle in another country?' 42 per cent of respondents replied 'yes' in March 1948. The respective percentages thereafter were 37 per cent in January 1948, 35 per cent in January 1950, 33 per cent in June 1951, 28 per cent in December 1955 and 41 per cent in January 1957.

Although only a small number of those persons who answered 'yes' to the pollsters' question actually emigrated, or even made enquiries about emigrating, the number of applications lodged at Australia House for assisted passages remained very high between 1947 and

1952. Furthermore, interest varied with the seasons and in response to political issues and crises which Britons believed could worsen their living conditions and cloud their futures. Cold, inclement weather in January and February, combined in the early post-war years with fuel-rationing, induced more Britons to lodge applications than did warm, sunny (though frequently wet) weather in July and August.

One of the first crises that produced a surge of interest in emigrating was the Western powers' airlift of food and other essentials to West Berlin. Many Britons obviously were afraid that the crisis would trigger another war in Europe. Then, during 1950–1, the United States became directly involved in the war between North and South Korea. Britain's expenditure on defence rose from 6 to 10 per cent of the gross national product, causing a slight decline in the standard of living. By 1950 rationing of foodstuffs had been reduced and the long-awaited return to normality seemed imminent. The perceived new crisis early in 1951 led many Britons who felt that they had 'had enough' to apply for assisted passages to Australia.

Only once during the period 1947–59 did the Australian government not actively encourage emigration from Britain. This was during the Australian economic recession of 1952–3. As part of a drastic general reduction in its immigration programme, Australia reduced its target for British migrants to 40,000. Australia House ceased advertising its Commonwealth Nomination Scheme and fewer applications were received in 1953 than in any earlier post-war year.

Although the level of interest in emigrating to Australia declined significantly between the 1952 recession and 1957, it rose in a most spectacular fashion as a result of the so-called Suez crisis. On 7 December 1956, *The Times* reported a rush of enquiries at the London emigration offices of Canada, New Zealand and Australia. A Canada House spokesman had told the *Times* correspondent that his office was dealing with four or five times as many enquiries about emigration to Canada as during the same period in 1955. In the fourth quarter of 1956 Australia House received double the number of letters of first enquiry that it had received in the same quarter in 1955. By early 1957, the rush of enquiries had developed into a stampede. The Canadian office reported handling 6000 medical reports each week, and prospective emigrants were queuing four-abreast outside Canada House. Similar queues gathered outside Australia House and continued for several hundred yards down the Strand. There is no doubt that many Britons believed that their government's involvement in the Suez affair could lead to a major confrontation and therefore a return to shortages and rationing, from which they had only recently been freed. In the first quarter of 1957 Australia House received 35,000 letters of first enquiry. Interest in the scheme was so great that the government again ceased advertising. Nor was the interest non-productive. During the same quarter, 14,750 application forms were received, compared with 8346 during the first quarter of 1956.

While there is no doubt that the crises stimulated interest in emigrating to Australia, there is also no doubt that they did not have a lasting impact on emigration. For example, on 6 December 1956 *The Times* reported that most of the people whom its correspondent had interviewed in the queues outside the Canadian and Australian offices had stated that their interest had been latent, that they had been thinking about emigrating for a long time and had decided to make definite enquiries because of the crisis. While the real motives of emigrants cannot be obtained simply by asking them one or two questions while they are standing in a queue, there is little doubt that the economic and political consequences, and expected consequences, of the Suez crisis – petrol rationing was reintroduced, the government hinted that it might increase taxation, and 40,000 workers were put on short time as a result of restrictions on oil and petrol supplies – contributed to a recrudescence of interest in emigration comparable with the interest shown in the first few years after the war.

Once the Suez crisis was over, the number of applications received by Australia House fell to a level insufficient to fill the quota of assisted passages. The decline in interest between 1957 and 1960 can be attributed mainly to greatly improved economic conditions in Britain. Expenditure on semi-luxury and luxury durables (radios, electrical goods, motor cars, and so on) rose sharply in 1959 to the highest post-war level, following a relaxation of restrictions on hire purchase – the so-called 'never never' scheme. The period was also free of the sort of political crises that had earlier stimulated a surge of interest in emigration.

The influence of improving economic conditions on emigration from a number of European countries had been noted by Australian officials since the early 1950s. To the 1953 Citizenship Convention, Harold Holt observed that on his recent visit to Europe he had found economic conditions much more prosperous than on a similar visit in 1948. A great deal of reconstruction had taken place, mainly as a result of financial aid from the United States. Furthermore, many European economies were buoyant as a result of hostilities in Korea. 'It was clear', said the Minister, 'that there was not the same strength of economic pressure impelling people to emigrate as was the case in the immediate post-war years . . . .' The same point was made to the 1955 Citizenship Convention by Pierre Jacobsen, Deputy Director of the Intergovernmental Committee for European Migration. The economic, political and psychological climate of Europe after the war, he said, had helped the Australian immigration programme by providing many thousands of persons anxious to leave Europe and to start a new life where freedom and political stability are in the very air one breathes. However, the European situation had changed markedly since those early post-war years. The economic recovery of the Federal Republic of Germany had been quite remarkable, and one of the most dynamic elements in that recovery had been the rapidly increasing demand for labour which had led Germany to become a country of net immigration. Harold Holt returned to the same theme during the 1956 Citizenship Convention. With improved conditions in European countries, including Britain, there was now rather less incentive for people to emigrate than there had been earlier. He therefore warned delegates that Australia cannot 'pick up the migrants when it is more convenient for us to do so. We may not have these opportunities indefinitely.'

A potential emigrant's conclusion that Australia offers a standard of living much higher than he is experiencing in Britain is probably calculated more by observation and judgement than by official indices of comparative standards of living. Such calculations are notoriously difficult to make, for not only is it necessary to estimate the purchasing power of expected compared with present income, but one also needs to take account of such things as housing size and facilities, climate, and opportunities for recreation. Because such factors are difficult to 'quantify', the potential emigrant will seldom, if ever, be in a position to calculate the real difference between his present and expected circumstances. In the first place, it is most unlikely that the necessary information will be available; and, in the second place, the potential emigrant may not know exactly where he will be living or employed and thus be unable to assess how much of his income will be expended on such items as housing, and travel to and from employment. There is also the question of 'necessities', which are by no means the same in

49

such vastly different countries. Warm clothing will be less necessary in Australia than in Britain, while ownership of a refrigerator and a private motor car is considered essential by many Australians (as was not the case in Britain in the 1950s).

Even so, a survey of British emigrants to Australia conducted in 1959–60 concluded that the real incomes of artisans and unskilled workers were much higher in Australia than in Britain. Average earnings were probably 28 per cent higher, and minimum wage rates for such skilled workers as fitters and turners, moulders, bootmakers, bricklayers and carpenters more than 50 per cent higher. The higher standard of living in Australia was also reflected in statistics which showed that ownership of houses, motor cars, refrigerators and washing machines was twice as high as in Britain. On the other hand, the incidence of direct taxes and social-service contributions and the provision of low-cost government housing were more favourable to families in Britain. Single persons in Britain were subject to a higher rate of direct taxation on their incomes than single persons in Australia, but the difference narrowed considerably for married couples with dependent children. For example, a British family with four dependent children whose net income did not exceed £1500 paid *less* tax than a family of similar size in Australia. In addition, the relative value of family allowances, maternity grants, unemployment and sickness benefits and widow's pensions was also higher in Britain. At that time, the British National Health Service also provided relatively cheaper and more comprehensive benefits than the Australian system of voluntary health insurance supplemented by government subsidies.

The survey concluded that, if the 28 per cent difference in average earnings (in Australia's favour) was adjusted for these outlays and corresponding remunerations, the difference for single males was increased to 39 per cent, the difference for a married couple with one child remained about the same (25–30 per cent depending on the age of the child) but the difference for a married couple with four dependent children was reduced to between 16 and 24 per cent. If the costs of resettling in Australia were added – for example, the replacement cost of housing, furniture and other durables, and the loss of seniority in employment – then the probable short-term economic gain from emigration to Australia by large families earning average or below-average incomes in Britain was not as great as had generally been assumed.

Who then were the British emigrants to Australia under the Assisted Passage Scheme and why did they go? Despite the fact that over a million Britons entered Australia during the life of the post-war scheme, very little is known about their backgrounds, their reasons for emigrating and what happened to them in Australia. The best source of information is the survey referred to above, conducted in 1959–60, when interest in emigration, as measured by the number of applications received at Australia House, had reached a post-war trough. Referred to hereafter as the Appleyard survey, it was based on interviews conducted with a sample of 862 British families and adult single persons a few weeks before they emigrated to Australia. As soon as an emigrant family (or individual) had been selected under the scheme, and told their vessel and date of departure, an interviewer associated with the project visited them in their home, where she sought answers to a number of questions about their reasons for emigrating and what they hoped to achieve in Australia. The interviews lasted two or more hours, and were conducted in as friendly and relaxed an atmosphere as possible. The results, published in *British Emigration to Australia* (1964), provide rare insights into the reasons why Britons responded to the Assisted Passage Scheme. And, while the results relate only to British assisted emigrants in 1959–60, they also reveal *processes* of decision-making which are probably typical of emigrants over the entire life of the scheme.

The general conclusion reached in the survey was that those Britons who emigrated to Australia in 1959–60 were by no means the ne'er-do-wells of British society. They were, first and foremost, a selected group: predominantly young families and single persons, only 8 per cent of whom were aged 45 years and over, compared with 37 per cent for the British population as a whole. The main reason for their youthfulness was that the Australian government invoked an age qualification in its selection of assisted emigrants which made it difficult for persons over 45 years old to obtain assisted passages unless they possessed exceptional qualifications, although the aged parents of children already settled in Australia were assisted on grounds that the family would be less likely to return to Britain if the parents joined them in Australia. The second major qualification invoked by the Australian government – occupational skill – had virtually been suspended at the time of the survey, because the number of persons registered for emigration at Australia House were barely sufficient to meet the 'targets' for 1959 and 1960. The government was therefore offering assisted passages to almost any Briton of appropriate age and in good health who applied.

Emigrants in the Appleyard survey were living in predominantly urban areas, usually on the suburban fringes of large cities and provincial towns. They were not over-represented in densely-populated conurbations. 54 per cent of families lived in detached and semi-detached houses and had the exclusive use of an average five rooms; 27 per cent lived in terraced dwellings with an average of 4.6 rooms. Of families who rented houses, 80 per cent paid less than £2 sterling per week, which represented on average about 15 – 20 per cent of their net weekly earnings.

An important finding of the survey was the relative absence of unemployed persons, even though it was taken when male unemployment was 3.2 per cent of the estimated workforce. Migration theory would have led one to expect a higher than average proportion of unemployed persons among the emigrants. However, Britain's very supportive social-security system had clearly led many unemployed or underemployed people to remain at home rather than risk the unknowns associated with resettlement in Australia. Indeed, only two of the 862 persons in the sample were unemployed at the time they made their decision to emigrate. Nor was there a predominantly high proportion of emigrants from such high-unemployment areas as Merseyside, Tyneside and Belfast.

From net incomes of about £13 sterling a week, for which they had worked an average 49 hours per week, emigrants had accumulated only modest assets. 44 per cent of families stated that they were not putting any of their current earnings into a savings bank or savings certificates. After selling most of their assets before departure, families expected to transfer an average £289, although those who owned or were buying their homes expected, after sale, to transfer an average £825. Predominantly Anglican or nonconformist by religion, the majority of husbands and wives had not continued their formal education beyond elementary level. The skills they possessed had generally been acquired through apprenticeship. The Assisted Passage Scheme in 1959 had not attracted many highly educated Britons. Nearly 80 per cent of married men had served in the forces during the Second World War and a large proportion of the younger males had done National Service training. Over 70 per cent of all males had travelled outside Britain either on military service or private visits. Although comparable data were not available for the whole British population of similar age, it seemed that overseas experience may well have been an important 'characteristic' of the emigrant compared with the non-emigrant population.

Why, then, did these young, employed, urban, well-housed families decide to emigrate from Britain with its very protective social-security system? Clues had been provided by two small surveys conducted with British emigrants to New Zealand and Australia just prior to the Appleyard survey. In 1953 L. B. Brown interviewed British single males who had enlisted with the Royal New Zealand Air Force after serving with the Royal Air Force and compared the results with those obtained from interviews with single British males who decided to re-enlist in the Royal Air Force. One of his major conclusions was that the emigrants had greater feelings of anxiety and responsiveness to their environment. A second study, conducted by Alan Richardson with Britons both intending and not intending to emigrate to Australia, showed that the intending migrants appeared to be more ambitious, more motivated, and more interested in action and hard work than non-migrants. They also had more energetic and outgoing personalities. In the Netherlands a similar study conducted by N. H. Frijda with Dutch emigrants to a number of overseas countries reached conclusions similar to those reached by Brown and Richardson. The emigrants were much more dissatisfied with life in Holland, showed less attachment to Dutch culture and were 'somewhat more enterprising' than non-emigrants.

In other words, the studies suggested that emigrants, when compared with non-emigrants of similar ages, social class and location, display a greater willingness to better themselves, were less prepared to accept their 'lot' without question, and were more enterprising and less attached to their culture. Indeed, one of the most distinguished scholars of migration, S. N. Eisenstadt, had already concluded that emigration is motivated by a feeling of 'insecurity and inadequacy' in a person's social setting. This feeling, he argued, may be due to a variety of reasons – overpopulation, declining economic opportunity, the opening-up of new cultural and economic horizons, and so on. Eisenstadt also argued that it is the existence of an objective opportunity that makes it possible for potential emigrants to realise their aspirations. The Appleyard survey was conducted with persons who had found that objective opportunity: emigration to Australia under the Assisted Passage Scheme.

In addition to the ready availability of assisted passages, the fact that Australia was a British country with a long tradition of warmly receiving immigrants from the 'old country' also influenced the decisions of many Britons who otherwise would not have emigrated or would have emigrated to some other country. Indeed, a survey conducted by the British government's *Social Survey* in 1966 showed that Australia was the favoured destination of most British families who had thought seriously about settling in another country. Two thirds of persons interviewed in that survey reported knowing someone who had emigrated and nearly 60 per cent of respondents knew someone who had emigrated to Australia. Such information led Alan Richardson to conclude that emigration was an acceptable form of behaviour in Britain and that settlement in Australia was the most likely goal of that behaviour.

Although many, perhaps most, of the persons who had emigrated to Australia under the Assisted Passage Scheme had the kind of enterprise and energetic personalities attributed to emigrants in general by Brown and Richardson, the ready availability of assisted passages also attracted many persons who otherwise may not have left Britain or who decided to go to Australia without commitment to settle. The cheap passage had only one substantial condition: that the emigrant remain in Australia for at least two years or repay to the Australian government the cost of his outward passage. Under these circumstances, many saw the scheme as an opportunity to spend a long working holiday in Australia or to escape difficult circumstances at home.

As already noted, the scheme provided for four types of assisted passage: (1) personally nominated migrants with relatives or employers in Australia who were prepared to nominate them, provide accommodation and assist with their early resettlement; (2) Commonwealth-nominated migrants who would be accommodated in Commonwealth hostels on their arrival in Australia; (3) single young persons for whom no accommodation arrangements had been made on grounds that they would be sufficently mobile to find a flat or boarding accommodation; (4) aged parents of migrants already in Australia who would go immediately to their sponsors' homes. It will be shown that both the motives for emigration and the decision-making processes differed considerably according to the type of assisted migrant.

All emigrants in the Appleyard survey were asked how long they had been thinking about emigrating before they decided to leave. 65 per cent of married couples had been thinking about emigrating for two years or longer, including 29 per cent who had taken longer than five years to reach their decisions. Personally nominated families took a slightly shorter time. The seed was often sown by an Australian or by someone who had been to Australia. Australian servicemen with whom the emigrant had served during the Second World War gave many respondents their first notion of emigrating. The following comment was typical: 'I worked a lot with Australians in the desert during the war and they talked a lot about Australia. It [emigration] has been in the back of my mind since then but we have been seriously considering it for about the last two years.' Australians who visited the United Kingdom and former emigrants who returned, including some who said that they did not like Australia but later changed their minds and hoped to re-emigrate, also generated considerable interest among potential emigrants. Quite a few emigrants were able to trace their initial interest in Australia to their childhood, and had sustained that interest for twenty or more years before they finally decided to go. The following is also a typical reply: 'At eleven I was interested by my uncle but my parents objected to my going to join him. We talked it over when we were married but the children prevented it by giving us other things to think about.' During the gestation period, emigrants generally obtained information from a number of sources. Obviously, relatives in Australia were the major source of information for personal nominees. Commonwealth nominees, on the other hand, had to rely on information from magazines, newspapers, books, films and so on.

Who nominated the personal nominees? Of the 400 personally nominated families, 283 had been nominated by former emigrants from Britain: 158 were members of the nominee's immediate family (brothers, sisters, parents, children) and 80 others were cousins, nephews, uncles. The remainder were friends and fiancés. About 65 per cent of the former-emigrant nominees had been in Australia for longer than three years.

A central tenet of economic theory concerning emigration is that, because individuals always act to maximise their real incomes, a potential emigrant, after calculating real income differences between his own and foreign countries, and the likely costs of travel, will choose the country which offers the highest real income for his skills. In the case of British emigration to Australia under the Assisted Passage Scheme, however, the offer of near-free travel led many migrants to consider only Australia, simply because they did not have the funds necessary to travel to other countries. Thus 406 of the 579 married couples in the survey had made no enquiries about emigrating to any other country. 70 had made enquiries about emigrating to New Zealand, 47 had considered Canada and 12 Rhodesia.

Personal responsibilities and commitments, including the wife's attachment to her parents, was a main reason why many families had stood at the emigration threshold for years before deciding to step across it. In fact, the parents of many migrants continued their opposition to the venture until the day their children left the country. Of the 452 wives who had either both parents or one parent living, 66 replied that at least one parent was strongly opposed to their emigration, and, although another 151 wives stated that their parents did not mind, their comments suggest they they really disapproved: 'They'll soon get over it, though they're not very happy just now' was a typical response.

Although family ties kept a majority of emigrants on the threshold, others would not have reached that threshold if they had not had relatives in Australia to make a personal nomination. Others said that they had not decided to move until they were satisfied that the cost of doing so justified the returns they expected in Australia. As already noted, many of the families were well housed, their average weekly earnings were slightly higher than average and they were covered by a very comprehensive social-services system. To these families the move to Australia involved the loss of job, accrued seniority and perhaps superannuation, and the loss of a house which may have taken years of waiting on a council list to secure. Yet, in spite of known and unknown difficulties associated with their departure and resettlement they had decided to take the plunge. It was not easy for them to decribe the forces and incidents which had led them to step across the emigration threshold. Many understandably showed a propensity to rationalise their reasons so as to make the case for going seem more logical than it really was. The decision, especially for Commonwealth-nominated families, was probably the most important of their married lives. Once taken, they tended to justify it by building a very favourable image of Australia and, contrariwise, an unfavourable image of Britain. Indeed, many emigrants gave the impression that they had deliberately avoided

London girls enquiring about the £10 passage at Australia House, London in 1956. (Photograph: Australian Dept. of Immigration, Canberra.)

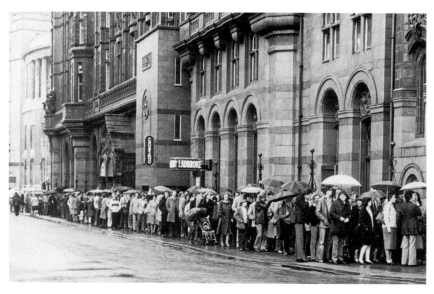

Thousands queued for hours to attend an Australian information day at Manchester on 8 March, 1981. (Photograph: Barry Pollitt.)

Doctors from London hospitals enquire about emigrating at Australia House following a protest in the Strand over working conditions and pay in Britain (2 June, 1970). (Photograph: Press Association.)

Entertainer Tommy Trinder bids farewell to a group of children from Dr. Barnardo's Village Home at Barkingside. The children were destined to live in three Dr. Barnardo's homes in New South Wales (20 March, 1956). (Photograph: Press Association.)

The Kinsella family of 14 fly to Australia under the Assisted Passage
Scheme (20 August, 1963). By the 1960s air travel played an important role
in the scheme. (Photograph: Press Association.)

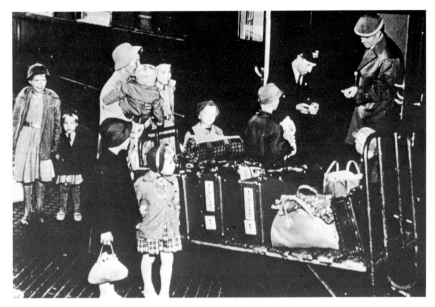

Assisted migrants leaving London, 1947 (Photograph: Australian Dept. of Immigration.)

The *Chitral*, a World War Two troop carrier, was converted by the Australian government to carry £10 immigrants to Australia. (Photograph: P & O.)

The dining room aboard the *Chitral*. Children and adults ate meals at separate sittings, while fixed seating arrangements led to the establishment of long-term friendships among immigrants. (Photograph: P & O.)

A dormitory cabin on the *Chitral*. Men and women were accommodated separately in large cabins like this in order to fit the maximum number of immigrants on the ships for each journey to Australia. (Photograph: P & O.)

The *Fairsea* arriving at Fremantle with British assisted migrants.
(Photograph: Australian Dept. of Immigration, Canberra.)

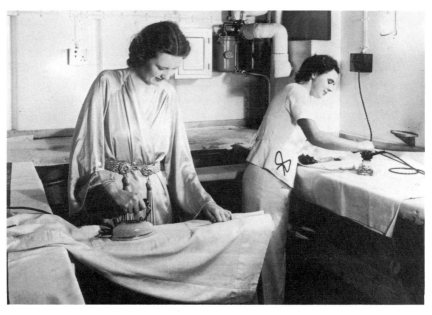

Women catching up on family chores aboard *Stratheden*. (Photograph: P & O.)

The type of accommodation many non-British migrants experienced during the 1940s and 1950s. (Photograph: *Herald & Weekly Times*, Melbourne.)

Otranto in Sydney harbour. (Photograph: National Library of Australia, Canberra.)

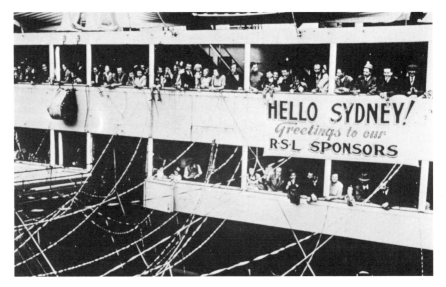

British migrants, sponsored by the Returned Servicemens League, arrive at Sydney, 1947.

A migrant hostel. (Photographs: Australian Dept. of Immigration, Canberra.)

seeking information about Australia once they had made their decision, in case the information tarnished the favourable image they had already established.

What, then, led people who had been standing on the threshold of emigration for so long to make the decision to cross it? The most common 'trigger' related to the work situation, the absence of prospects for advancement and perceived limited prospects for their children if they remained in Britain. Events such as being placed on short time in their employment or disappointments concerning housing were common triggers for an application to emigrate under the Assisted Passage Scheme. The trigger must not be confused with having thought seriously about emigrating to Australia or elsewhere. The trigger was invariably the last straw in a series of frustrations which finally led people who had been on the threshold for many years to decide finally to go. Sometimes it was not even a specific incident:

> I'm working a bare 44 hour week just now with no overtime or bonus and I have been for the past nine months, so it's really a hand-to-mouth existence and, with my boy coming to the age when he'll be leaving school soon, I can't see any prospect of him getting a decent job here, as good jobs for young fellows are hard to get. So I've decided to make a move both for his sake and for our own, as I am a young man yet and good for another twenty years' work out there.

This emigrant touched on the main reason given by most emigrants: better opportunities for themselves and their children. Other 'reasons', such as better climate, could be classified as supplementary. The nexus between 'primary' and 'secondary' reasons was usually as follows: the decision to emigrate was basically economic in motivation and was made after a long stay on the emigration threshold. During this period, numerous forces pushed and pulled the emigrant, but none was strong enough to make him take a step forwards or backwards. Finally, some new incident of frustration, or perhaps the offer of employment and housing in Australia which had not been previously made, led him to take the step. Climate, open space and the prospect of better health were important components working in Australia's favour, but they were not the primary reasons given by many families.

The interviews with families were conducted with both husband and wife together. This provided them with opportunity to discuss, or even disagree, with each other concerning the reasons why they were going. It was common for the husband to have had the first thought about emigrating, often as a result of contact with Australian servicemen and the difficulty of settling down into civvy life after five or more years in the services. But shortly after the war he married and, for one reason or another, his wife had no desire to leave Britain. The husband, however, was well and truly established on the emigration threshold, prepared to emigrate at any time. By 1959, their eldest child was in secondary school and would enter the workforce in 1961 or 1962, followed by several others in, say, alternate years. Their eldest children were, in fact, part of the demographic 'bulge' of the early post-war years, a phenomenon which parents expected would make 'good jobs' difficult to find. The expected effect of the bulge was specifically mentioned by many parents whose main reason for emigrating was better opportunities for their children. Thus, the bridegroom of 1946 who had been unable to convince his bride that they should start a new life together in Australia was able, fourteen years later, to convince her that it would be a good move because if the children stayed in Britain they would not find good jobs. If the family lived in one of the coal or textile towns where the husband faced redundancy, and if they had a close relative who had emigrated to Australia after the war, had done well and was prepared to nominate them, the decision to emigrate was not difficult to reach.

There is also no doubt that many emigrants believed that Britain's social structure and class system would prevent their children from fulfilling their potential. As children of working-class parents, many emigrants believed that their children would begin the race to the 'top' under a considerable social hardship. Although very few emigrants stated that the British class system was a reason for their emigration, many families, especially the large families, said that their own limited opportunities for a good education and their working-class background had restricted their achievements and that the same barriers would restrict their children's achievements. Australia, they said, was a sort of classless society where everyone, irrespective of school or family background, had an equal opportunity and where ability was the only criterion of promotion.

The Appleyard survey concluded that the level of dissatisfaction (especially the absence of opportunities for advancement for themselves and their children) was generally higher for Commonwealth nominees than for personal nominees. Not only did the former not know anyone in Australia who was prepared to nominate them, but they didn't even know their port of disembarkation in Australia. This would be decided by officials a few days before their ship reached Fremantle and would depend mainly on current employment opportunities and hostel accommodation in each state. Thus, on arrival, a family might be told to remain on the vessel for another week and disembark at Melbourne or Sydney. The family also faced the near-certain prospect of a year at least in a hostel, and, while most put on a brave face about this daunting prospect, they knew that it would be a severe test of their character, their relationship and their commitment to making a success of the new life in Australia. Commonwealth nominees, generally semi-skilled workers and their wives with three or more children and only £300 in their pockets when they embarked can be aptly described as the modern pioneers.

Personal nominees, on the other hand, would go to the homes of their close relatives, where they would receive a great deal of assistance and support during the first few weeks, including assistance in finding accommodation and employment and advice on how to react and adjust to the values and expectations of Australian society. Only a few personal nominees had been warned by their relatives of any difficulties that they might encounter during their first few months in Australia. Perhaps the emigrants had read a great deal more into the letters received by their nominators than was actually written, because almost all of them discounted the difficulties of adjustment simply because their relatives would be around to lend a hand.

The majority of young single men and women in their 'teens and early twenties who emigrated to Australia had been given the rare opportunity to travel to the other side of the world for less than the cost of a weekend in Paris. None doubted their ability to save the cost of a return passage if, after two years in Australia, they decided to return to Britain. Nurses and teachers were over-represented in the survey because their qualifications were accepted in Australia, where there were many employment opportunities for them. With more candour than most families, and with no reason to justify their decisions, many of the young single girls felt that they were simply in a 'rut' and wanted a change.

Whatever their decision-making processes or their propensity to rationalise their decisions, nearly all respondents were optimistic about their chances of succeeding in Australia. What Britain lacked, Australia possessed in abundance. It was a land where anyone could succeed. This comment of a 30-year-old married man from Derbyshire was typical: 'The prospects are better there for anyone with a country that's really just starting to breathe. There must be good prospects – they're still pioneering. I think Australia will be *the* country in years to come when they have expanded and developed.' Another spoke for many when she said that 'the freer way of life, open air, the climate, the fact that everyone has an equal chance if they're willing to work' was the reason why she believed that her family would make a success of the venture.

The Appleyard survey also explored with emigrants their expectations and knowledge of Australia. It had been argued that if emigrants had a good knowledge of Australia then the chances of their expectations being fulfilled would be greater. The questions asked emigrants were based on information from booklets on many aspects of Australian society that were given to each assisted emigrant when he/she lodged an application. In summary, the quiz revealed that emigrants knew a great deal more about those aspects of Australia which were likely to have a direct bearing on their resettlement (for instance, wage rates, hours worked, taxation rates and family allowances) than about Australia's geography and politics. Thus, their expectations for wages were generally not extravagant because they had taken the trouble to find out the going rates. Most of the emigrants, especially the skilled workers, intended finding employment of the type they had in Britain. Furthermore, only 17 per cent of the emigrants planned, in due course, to become entrepreneurs; most intended to remain employees. At the time of interview 39 per cent of wives were working, but 62 per cent said they planned to work in Australia so that the family would be able to purchase a house as soon as possible.

Home-ownership was one of their central expectations. Not only did 80 per cent of families mention it, but nearly all of these had already had clear ideas about the size of the dwelling they would acquire (number of rooms), how much it would cost, how long it would be before they could sign the purchase agreement, and the period of mortgage. Only a minority of families had seriously overestimated how soon they would be able to put down a deposit; the expectations of the majority were quite realistic.

Large, Commonwealth-nominated families who were destined to

spend perhaps a year or more in a hostel displayed excellent knowledge of those economic conditions which would have an important bearing on their resettlement. Single persons knew very little about Australia; for most it really was a long working holiday and, aside from a fairly accurate knowledge of wage rates, they had failed to absorb other information provided by Australia House.

The Appleyard survey showed that British assisted emigrants to Australia in 1959–60 were not the ne'er-do-wells of British society, pushed out by poverty and inability to cope with problems at home. They tended to be slightly more skilled than the average British worker, much younger and well housed. Both personal and Commonwealth nominees had generally been thinking about emigrating for three to five years before they decided to go. The degree of crisis that led to the decision was greater for Commonwealth than for personal nominees. One of the most important conclusions of the Appleyard survey was that very few emigrants planned to become entrepreneurs. Emigration afforded the opportunity to better their socio-economic conditions rather than change their socio-economic status. They were not people who planned to build empires in the Antipodes; indeed, very few of them planned to change their occupations. To purchase a house, educate their children and live in a society free of class-based restrictions on achievement were the main objectives of their venture.

Chapter 5

Departure, Voyage and the New Life

The final stage in the selection process was for the family to be inteviewed by an Australian selection officer and to undergo a medical examination. As they would not have been called for interview had their application forms not shown that they had met the main selection criteria, the interview was essentially an exercise in confirmation. Most migrants, however, took it very seriously. They arrived well before time, dressed in their best outfits, the children having been pre-warned of dire consequences if they misbehaved. Although selection officers encouraged the families to ask questions about any aspect of life in Australia, few in fact did so. They had already decided to go, and to express doubts or ignorance at that crucial stage might, they thought, count against them. Their answers to the fairly bland questions asked by selection officers tended to exude enthusiasm for everything Australian. Few missed the opportunity to say that they wanted to succeed and, of course, become 'good Australians'. Experienced selection officers were quick to discover whether both spouses were equally enthusiastic about the venture. Experience had shown that, if the wife in particular had reservations, then the difficulties ahead, specially if they were Commonwealth nominees, would probably be considerable. In such cases, the wife was often given special counselling.

Provided there were no hitches in these formal proceedings, the family would receive a letter of selection within a few days followed later by notification of their date of departure. As cargo space on migrant vessels was limited, emigrants were asked to take only personal effects. Thus furniture and most household goods had to be sold. As the period between notification and departure was about six weeks, possessions acquired over many years had to be sold in a hurry, which meant that they were usually sold at bargain prices. Many of the emigrants in the Appleyard survey, especially those living in provincial towns where demand for secondhand furniture was not high, reported calling in a dealer who offered them 'a hundred pounds for the lot'. Many items were given to relatives; others were sold through advertisements in local papers. Home-owners had the additional problem of selling their houses in an unreasonably short period. Some refused to accept the offers made by agents and asked their relatives to handle the sale after they had left.

The sale of furniture and homes under 'buyer's market' conditions remained a sore point with many migrants for years thereafter. Replacement cost of these items in Australia proved to be many times the price they had obtained from the sale of their possessions in Britain. The six weeks before departure were, without any doubt, a period of great stress for the emigrants. The consequences of their decision were manifest every day. The husband had to give notice of resignation to an employer for whom he may have worked for years; at farewell parties his mates said they respected him for the guts he had shown in deciding to leave his home for an unknown future on the other side of the earth. The period was especially stressful for children, who had to sever, perhaps for ever, close friendships at school and in the neighbourhood. Leaving the only environment they had every known, and giving away such precious possessions as a bike because it could not be taken, caused many youngsters to cry themselves to sleep in the room where they had thought their most private thoughts and kept their most treasured possessions. On one of the several journeys I made on migrant vessels during the early 1960s I was told by a ten-year-old girl that her most lasting impression of leaving Britain was seeing the family's possessions – two tea chests and six suitcases – stacked in the front room of their empty home awaiting the local carrier to take it to the railway station. Two tea chests, six suitcases and perhaps a bank transfer of £300 were the lifetime possessions that the family of six were taking to Australia.

Wives characteristically were much less enthusiastic about emigrating than their husbands, and so the last six weeks severely tested their resolve and, in many ways, their marriages. Again, the test was greatest for Commonwealth nominees. The unknowns in the venture were enormous. Few wives had travelled abroad; most had lived all their lives in one town or county. They had no idea how they would cope with shipboard life, in which part of Australia they would settle, and what hostel life would be really like. For the vague promise of better opportunities for their husband and children, they were now dismantling all aspects of the only way of life they knew. Nor could the cheerful farewells of lifelong neighbours who gathered to see them depart for the station ever compensate for the sadness wrought by their last glimpse of an empty home.

Many families were accompanied by their close relatives to London, from where the migrant trains took them to either Tilbury or Southampton. Here again, they experienced another occasion of great sadness. As the train slowly pulled out of the station, close relatives who had come to see them off moved at the same pace along the platform, waving, shouting encouragement and good wishes. When the platform ended they stopped; but the train steamed on. For both emigrants and their relatives it was a moment of great agony. Parents who honestly believed that they might never see their children and grandchildren again walked slowly and tearfully back along the platform. The emigrant family, trying hard to fight back their tears, stared impassively through the carriage window as they left behind virtually everything that meant home to them.

The allocation of ship and cabin to an assisted migrant was something of a lottery. Under arrangements with P & O and other British shipping companies, a block of cabins on each liner sailing to Australia had been booked in advance by the Australian government. Migrant families who travelled on these vessels were allocated tourist-class cabins to themselves, depending upon the ages of their children. They had access to all the facilities available to other tourist passengers; their meals were typically British dishes and, perhaps more important, the many non-assisted passengers, both British and Australian, could provide them with encouragement and advice about resettling in Australia. On the other hand, those who were allocated berths on *Fairsea* and *Fairsky*, converted carrier escorts owned by the Italian Sitmar Line, were less fortunate; these ships were smaller than P & O vessels and therefore less stable in rough weather; all the passengers were assisted migrants, and the crew, including galley staff, were Italian. Many migrants were unable to adjust to these conditions.

65

Thus, the experience of a personally nominated assisted family who were allocated a four-berth cabin on P & O's *Arcadia*, and who on disembarking at Sydney after a three-week voyage were met by the wife's brother, with whom they stayed for six weeks, was very different from the experience of a Commonwealth-nominated family allocated a cabin on Sitmar's *Fairsea*, told after three weeks that they would eventually be disembarked at Melbourne, and accommodated in a hostel. Yet, for both families, the third in that trilogy of farewells – home, railway station and shipside – had an awesome impact. Once the last ropes had been untied and the vessel glided slowly into the harbour, they were truly emigrants. Until that moment, they could change their minds. The next stop was Port Said, Egypt. Indeed, officials always became a little apprehensive if the vessel's departure was delayed, for experience had shown that at least two or three emigrants would change their minds and rush down the gangway.

A salient feature of travel on migrant ships was that each family *had* to make new friendships. Sometimes these were initiated by allocation to a mealtime sitting at a specific table. Many lifelong friendships were begun at the first meal, although the Bay of Biscay could usually be counted upon to keep many emigrants in their bunks until calmer Mediterranean seas were reached. The routine of shipboard life became increasingly attractive; friendships were consolidated in an atmosphere devoid of responsibilities save for the need to keep an eye on the children. Some vessels had crèches; others arranged for passengers with teaching skills to organise classes during the mornings. Meals for children were provided separately and earlier than for parents, and with a little juggling the parents could arrange for the children to be asleep by the time they dined. Deck sports were arranged during the day, and dances, bingo and films at night. And, on three occasions at least, the ship stopped at such places as Port Said, Suez, Aden and Colombo, where many migrants disembarked and experienced for the first time cultures and ways of life known only through books and films. Aden, then a free port, was the place where many emigrants spent more than they should have on cheap radios, watches and jewellery. Indeed, the £300 that the average migrant took with him was usually much depleted by the time he reached Australia. Foreign ports and cheap duty-free drinks, available at all times on the ship, provided temptations that few could resist.

Yet, ever present during this period of enjoyment was the knowledge that every day brought them closer to the reality of their decision. Welfare officers, placed on board migrant vessels to provide information and to answer questions, frequently reported that their offices were visited by many more migrants during the last few days out of Fremantle than during the five or six days in the Mediterranean. Many of the questions posed were ones to which the migrants already had answers; all they needed was confirmation.

Arrival at Fremantle, the small port of Perth on the western side of Australia, after three or four weeks at sea was an event anticipated greatly by all emigrants. For most, the official literature on costs, wages and social security, and the brochures on Australia's landscape, had not adequately prepared them for arrival at the first Australian port. Fremantle is still, to some degree, inhabited by very friendly people who think nothing of stopping newcomers in the street and asking them if they can be of any assistance. Their own experience of this confirmed for many migrants what they had heard about Australians, and refuted what others had heard about Australians' dislike of Pommies. Many emigrants took a coach tour of Perth and its environs, where they saw, and generally approved, their first Australian landscape, so different from the sandy, bleak appearance of the coast from shipside. One enterprising coach operator, who knew that emigrants on the Sitmar vessels longed for British-type food, completed his tour of the city at a tearooms in Fremantle and suggested to his charges that, after a pot of tea and scones, they return to the ship via the fish markets, where fish and chips could be procured. Waterside workers still talk about the dozens of British migrants returning from the fish shop along the wharf, happily munching fish and chips wrapped in newspaper.

The consensus about Fremantle, discussed at great length during the remainder of the voyage across the Great Australian Bight, was that it looked like a town out of some Wild West movie: wide streets, swinging doors to the entrances of hotels, and footpaths protected by verandahs. However, discussion also centred on more serious matters. The Commonwealth nominees had already been told their fate by officials; the personal nominees had received letters from their relatives saying how much they were looking forward to the reunion. With each day, the real beginning of the new venture came closer.

As expected, the personal nominees were met by their nominators, generally relatives whom they had not seen for many years. Family and goods were packed into a trailer behind the car and, midst incessant conversation about the health of old friends, interspersed with information about buildings and landscape and, more important, about arrangements already made for employment and perhaps housing, the families headed for the nominator's home in an outer suburb. Showing off possessions he had accumulated since his arrival in Australia with packages similar to the ones brought by his newly arrived relatives was understandable behaviour by the nominator. In some ways, his achievement discouraged the newcomers; in others, it showed what could be achieved in a short time in the land of plenty. Sleeping arrangments had to be reorganised: two bedrooms in a three-bedroom house were generally allocated to the adults and perhaps small infants; the other bedroom and perhaps beds on a verandah or porch were shared by the nominator's children and their newly discovered cousins.

These were exciting times: the makeshift arrangements, far from being an imposition, were for most families, especially the children, an occasion of great happiness. However, in such circumstances, the secret of success was not to continue the makeshift arrangement for too long. Employment of the newcomer posed few problems; early 1960 was a period of full employment in Australia, and if he was skilled the newcomer could often choose from a number of job vacancies.

Housing was another matter. As already noted, its shortage in Australia had been caused by the cessation of housing construction during the war. Post-war marriages, and the arrival of hundreds of thousands of migrants, had prevented the supply of new houses, or the availability of old ones, from meeting housing demand. Rented accommodation was practically unavailable, and the waiting lists for State Housing Commission dwellings (equivalent to council houses in Britain) were measured in years. While it was less difficult to purchase a house, banks and other lending institutions, short of money in a period of very rapid economic growth, were insisting that clients provide a deposit of about £A1500 to qualify for a loan to purchase a plot of land on which a three-bedroom dwelling could be constructed. Migrants in the Appleyard survey, as already seen, brought much less money than that. Obtaining a job and saving as much as possible was therefore a prime objective of the newcomer. Most of the wives who said they planned to work, and many who didn't, entered the workforce so that the so-called housing 'deposit gap' could be breached more rapidly. Numbers and ages of children generally influenced the wife's decision to work. Some wives with several dependent children could or would not seek paid employment; others tried their hand at part-time jobs if the hours coincided with school hours.

The knowledge, support and advice of the nominator were of central importance for personal nominees during their early months in Australia. Simple things such as making his car available so that the newcomers could be first to answer an advertisement for a rented house, telling all his friends about his relatives' needs, and, in some cases, renovating unused buildings (such as a garage or shed) or allowing his relatives to park a caravan on his property, were of great assistance in easing the problems of resettlement.

Commonwealth nominees, on the other hand, had none of these benefits. On their arrival at Sydney or Melbourne, families were generally loaded onto buses which headed for a specific hostel. Allocation of hostel depended partly on availability of accommodation and partly on the husband's skill. For example, if he was a skilled fitter and turner and had already been offered a job in an industrial centre in an outer suburb, then he and his family would be allocated accommodation at the nearest hostel with available accommodation. While the journey they made through inner suburbs may have been along a route similar to the journey taken by a personal nominee, the impact of arrival was as different as anyone could imagine. Migrant hostels were generally ex-army camps or warehouses converted to accommodate migrant families. No one, least of all government officials, considered hostels adequate for anything other than a short transitional period, but, as will be shown, and as the Citizenship Convention had been told in 1957, some families stayed there for more than two years. The accommodation was as stark and spartan as the buildings themselves. Many families literally gasped at their first sight of the hostel; a few stood firm and refused to enter; others burst into tears as they followed their children to the rooms they had been allocated. Indeed, the arrival of a busload of newcomers at the hostel was often greeted by shouts of 'You'll be sorry!' from the long-term residents!

The luckier Commonwealth nominees were sent to hostels comprising Nissen huts each of which was shared with one other family, although privacy was maintained only tenuously by a flimsy partition between the two sets of lodgings. Those accommodated in converted warehouses sometimes found themselves in rooms whose walls ended in mid air; without ceilings, the roof of the warehouse could be seen 40 or so feet above the bed. Other converted warehouses, with fibreboard ceilings, were more comfortable and private. All migrants ate together in a communal dining hall and shared wash-rooms, showers and toilets. Families who had lived in separate dwellings in Britain were required to make enormous adjustments in order to cope with hostel life. The wife's role was especially difficult. If she had several children of school and pre-school ages, she was unable to take paid employment, unable to exercise her domestic role as cook and provider of meals, and, especially irksome, had to share bathrooms and toilets with dozens of persons unknown. In winter, the cold, unheated, warehouse-type hostels were especially uncomfortable. Some families tried to alleviate the monotony of communal meals by cooking in their rooms on hotplates, but this was forbidden and offenders were upbraided by the authorities and warned that they could be evicted.

Husbands escaped the hostel environment for most of the day, but on their return understandably bore the wrath of wives who, after having sent children to school and spent the day caring for their pre-school children in an environment so different from the home in Britain, badgered them to do everything possible to get the family out of what they called 'the prison'. Escape was also the main topic of conversation of wives who gathered together during the day while their husbands were at work and their children were at school. The camaraderie that developed among them was born of common difficulties and disappointments. Many of the hostels were a long way from shopping centres or from railway stations where wives could have travelled to the cities. But this would not have been that much of a help. The simple fact was that most of them knew nobody in Australia except the wives of others in the same situation. The hostel accommodation took a large proportion of the husband's wage, and so saving rapidly in order to breach the 'deposit gap' was as difficult as being first to answer an advertisment for a house if you did not own a motor car. Many hostels employed housing officers to assist migrants, but, in view of the market conditions and the migrants' low savings and capacity to save, the officers' advice was largely academic.

The Commonwealth nominee, wrote Nightingale, looked out at Australia from a community of immigrants living a pseudo-communal life in a sub-standard ex-army camp or warehouse – an often squalid ghetto isolated from both the Australian people and places of employment, and therefore a ripe environment in which disillusionment and discontent could fester. Richardson, a social psychologist, who with

Nightingale analysed data collected by the Appleyard team during follow-up interviews in 1961 and 1967 with the emigrants he had first seen before they left Britain in 1959–60, had insights into other aspects of the hostel experience. Sometimes, he wrote, families stayed in a hostel because they felt more secure among their compatriots. The world outside could seem too threatening, and, the longer they remained, the less inclined they were to risk any deeper financial and emotional involvement in Australian life.

The Appleyard team decided to conduct follow-up interviews with the 862 families and single persons 18-20 months after their arrival in Australia. The choice of period was deliberate. Statistics and field research had shown that a high proportion of returning migrants left Australia between two years and two years three months after arrival, i.e. when they had been in Australia for the two years they had to stay in order to avoid having to repay the government the cost of their outward passages. As one of the main reasons for conducting the Appleyard survey was to try to understand the resettlement processes of British assisted migrants, including why so many migrants returned, it was decided to conduct reinterviews within two years of their arrival.

As in Britain, interviews were conducted with families in their homes (or hostels). Over two to three hours, newcomers were given the opportunity not only to answer questions about their achievements relative to their original expectations but also to ruminate about the problems of settling into Australian society. Arrangements were then made for second follow-up interviews to be conducted in 1967 with as many of the migrants as possible, including those who had returned to Britain or emigrated to another country. These interviews provided a great deal of valuable information on all aspects of the settlement of British migrants in Australia. A third and final set of interviews is planned for 1989–90, when many of the original migrants will have retired, shifting the focus to the achievements of their children, grandchildren and, in several instances, great-grandchildren.

Nightingale the economist and Richardson the social psychologist not only worked closely with me during the follow-up surveys but also published separate volumes on economic and social aspects of the migrants' resettlement. The remainder of this chapter, and chapters 6 and 7, report and summarise important aspects of the resettlement process, successful or otherwise, of the sample of assisted migrants who had left Britain in 1959–60.

'Higher and more reliable earnings', 'better living standards', 'better housing' and 'better opportunities for the children' were phrases used by almost every emigrant as a main reason for deciding to leave for Australia. The follow-up interviews conducted in 1961 and 1967, the crucial six-year period during which a migrant's resettlement is consolidated, indicate the extent to which their expectations were fulfilled. Their arrival in Australia preceded by a few months a minor economic recession. Although the recession was short-lived, it caused seasonally adjusted unemployment to rise from 1 per cent to 2.7 per cent of the estimated Australian workforce between the last quarters of 1960 and 1961. Thereafter, full employment was reachieved and the 1960s became known as Australia's economic golden years, when hundreds of thousands of immigrants, British and non-British, arrived and found immediate employment.

The wages that the sampled British migrants earned in their first jobs in Australia were much higher than the wages they had earned in their last jobs in Britain, and also represented a significant, once-and-for-all gain in *real* income. Thereafter, their incomes increased in line with those of other wage and salary earners in Australia. Furthermore, during the early 1960s their incomes increased at a faster rate than those of workers with similar skills who remained in Britain. Lacking furniture and other consumer durables when they arrived, the migrants' highest priority in disposing of their new, higher incomes was for the purchase of furniture, motor cars, washing machines and television sets, goods that could be acquired immediately and were, of course, essential if they had been lucky enough to obtain rented unfurnished houses. Some gave top priority to the purchase of a motor car, so that they could not only reach rented accommodation as soon as it was advertised, but – especially if they were in poor accommodation such as hostels – get out and about to see and enjoy the Australian countryside. Those who had brought to Australia only a few hundred pounds capital generally acquired most of their durables under hire-purchase agreements.

It was during this early period that migrants particularly lamented the sale of their furniture in Britain for such a small total return. Their incomes in Australia may have been substantially higher, but they soon discovered that prices of durables were also higher, a situation exacerbated both by high rate of economic growth and by the similar requirements of hundreds of thousands of other newcomers. Furthermore, items such as refrigerators and cars, unnecessary (and financially unattainable) in Britain, were soon seen as essential in Australia, just as those migrants who settled in the north of the continent found heating and warm clothes unnecessary. By the end of the six-year period, almost all migrants, whether personal or Commonwealth nominees, who were still in Australia owned all the necessary furniture and consumer durables.

While early acquisition of televisions, motor cars and refrigerators was deemed important and necessary, the problems in obtaining them were minor compared with those of acquiring ownership of a dwelling. This, of course, had stood high among the expectations of all immigrants before they left Britain. Almost every family, whether or not they had owned a house in Britain, said that they hoped to acquire one in Australia. While their expectations were, with few exceptions, achieved, the road to achievement differed considerably between families. As one would expect, the road travelled by Commonwealth nominees during their early years in Australia was especially rocky. Personal nominees generally spent a much shorter period in their initial accommodation (i.e. boarding with relatives) than Commonwealth nominees in hostels: about half of them stayed less than three months with their nominator, but 36 per cent of Commonwealth nominees were still in hostels when reinterviewed in 1961, i.e. about 18 months after they had arrived in Australia. As would be expected, all families (both Commonwealth and personal nominees) were on average far worse off for living space in their initial accommodation than they had been in their last home in Britain.

For Commonwealth nominees, living in a hostel 'not fit for humans to live in', 'very unsuitable for children', socially isolating and 'full of "odd" people', where they had little personal contact with the wider Australian community, clearly hampered their ability to establish a normal household. One of the major problems was that the cost of living in the hostel consumed up to 80 per cent of the family's income, especially if the wife had to remain in the hostel and care for pre-school and school children. This left the family with a greatly reduced capacity to save rapidly for the deposit necessary to acquire a house. Concessionary tariffs applied where the income of the migrant was deemed insufficient to meet minimum social needs after the payment of board. However, once the breadwinner was employed, he was subject to additional levies for miscellaneous charges such as excess electricity.

Understandably, many migrants used some of the income not spent on board to travel away from the hostel environment as frequently as possible. Most families, especially those with only one income-earner, therefore found it almost impossible to save the deposit required for a house. As already noted, their chances of obtaining rented accommodation were very low.

Personal nominees generally paid far less for board to their relatives than Commonwealth nominees paid to the hostels. Some paid only nominal board, and even those who had to pay the full cost were better off than Commonwealth nominees. Even so, many experienced difficulties if they stayed too long or were disinclined to humble themselves to a relative or in-law they had never really liked. One respondent spoke for many when he told the interviewer of events which had led to a 'falling-out' with his wife's relatives after the first six weeks. It was fine at first, he said, but, when the cousins came to blows over what seemed to be trivial matters (such as sharing of toys) and he resented his brother-in-law's persistent, overbearing manner, he took his family to live in a nearby caravan park.

At the time of the first follow-up survey, in 1961, it was clear that a large number of Commonwealth nominees had found great difficulty in leaving the hostel, whereas a good many personal nominees had moved from their initial accommodation within weeks of their arrival. It is therefore hardly surprising that, when asked about their housing conditions relative to those they had enjoyed in Britain, a much higher proportion of Commonwealth than of personal nominees said it was far worse. Furthermore, given the difficult circumstances of hostel life, only 10 per cent of Commonwealth nominees had managed to purchase a dwelling – a much lower proportion than for personal nominees. This 10 per cent included some very remarkable people. For example, one family living in a hostel in Melbourne decided to use their small savings to acquire a secondhand car. Every morning at the crack of dawn, before going to work, the husband would hurry off to check advertisements for rented accommodation that appeared in the morning newspaper, which he often collected from the newspaper's city office at 3 a.m. Such accommodation, if available, tended to be in outer, near-rural parts of Melbourne. Undaunted by persistent disappointment and realising that his morning journeys were taking him increasingly further from the hostel, he finally succeeded in obtaining accommodation at an old farmhouse at Digger's Rest. The dwelling, which had been acquired by the owner of a neighbouring property, was being used to store hay. After spending a lot of time making the farmhouse habitable, the family loaded their car with the possessions they had brought from England and made for the new home in which they lived for many years. Although the husband showed all the traits that Richardson and others have found typical of emigrants – ambition, motivation and hard work – few other migrants responded to their housing problems in quite such a determined way. Many became overwhelmed by hostel life and some soon decided that the most viable option was to return to Britain as soon as they stayed for two years.

Many migrants, though not the majority, moved temporarily into rented accommodation of a standard lower than they said they would be prepared to tolerate in the long term: caravans, garages (while building on their plot of land), weatherboard or fibro cottages which they judged to be of far inferior standard to their dwellings they had vacated in Britain. The number of rooms to which migrant families had exclusive use increased considerably between arrival and the first follow-up survey. Even so, nearly two thirds said that they now had the use of fewer rooms than they had had in Britain. Many migrants were also critical of the quality of Australian housing and facilities. Typical comments were that the houses had been constructed with inferior materials (weatherboard and fibro), that heating in winter and insulation in summer were inadequate, that houses in the outer suburbs of the cities did not have mains sewerage, that drainage was inadequate and that rooms were smaller. The only consistent favourable comment pertained to the relatively large and useful gardens. Migrants also complained about the absence of footpaths and kerbing on their streets, the infrequency of public transport, and the long journeys they had to make if they worked in the city.

Those renting houses at first follow-up paid an average rent of between 15 and 20 per cent of their household income (i.e. incomes earned by husband and wife). While this was not high by Australian standards, it should be noted that 70 per cent of householders in Australia live in dwellings which they either own or are purchasing. Rented housing is therefore in short supply. Thus many newcomers, irrespective of their aspirations for housing before departure, were forced to buy a house because of the market situation. 31 per cent of emigrants had been home-owners in Britain. By the time of the first follow-up, one third of personal nominees, but only one fifth of

Commonwealth nominees, had fulfilled their plans for home-owner-ship. Over one half of Commonwealth nominees had already aban-doned such plans. This reflected their higher levels of dissatisfaction compared with personal nominees, their greater isolation and perhaps a higher propensity to return to Britain. The survey therefore revealed that nearly one third of the emigrants who had decided before emigrating to buy a house in Australia had already abandoned their plans within two years of arrival, despite the very high social value placed by migrants on home-ownership in Australia.

There is little doubt that the first 18 months to two years is the most difficult period for an immigrant. The Appleyard survey clearly showed that the search for permanent housing was by no means over for most migrants after 18 months. Personal nominees were certainly in a much better position by this time than Commonwealth nominees, more having moved into permanent residences where they were enjoying the use of better housing than they had had in Britain. By contrast, many Commonwealth nominees were still in the ghetto atmosphere of the hostel, few were satisfied and most regarded their accommodation as much worse than the housing they had left behind. The fact that only a few of the relatively better-off migrants in hostels had taken steps to purchase a house probably reflects the debilitating effect of hostels on their aspirations.

What had the emigrants achieved by the time of the second follow-up survey, in 1967? Of the families still residing in Australia, 58 per cent owned or were buying their own houses, which is lower than the 70 per cent for the population in general. Only one quarter of the migrants had not moved since the first follow-up survey and nearly a third had moved three or more times. The survey showed a clear and direct relationship between the amount of capital migrants had initially brought to Australia and their purchase of housing, although the relationship also depended on family composition and the stage reached in the family's life cycle. Those migrants who transferred above-average amounts of capital were more likely to have bought houses in Australia during the first six years than those who had transferred below-average amounts. While the large majority of migrants with high capital transfers had been home-owners in Britain, Nightingale concluded that a more innate characteristic of emigrants who had bought houses was their higher propensity to save. This depended not only on the household income relative to need, but also on the personality traits of husband and wife – thrifty or spendthrift, clever or ineffectual budgeters – and on the relationships between the family members.

The typical type of dwelling acquired by migrants was a detached bungalow constructed either of brick or of other materials. Semi-detached and terraced houses had been acquired by less than 10 per cent of the migrants and only a few were living in flats. Their dwellings typically had three or four bedrooms and were generally thought to be more spacious and comfortable than their former homes in Britain. However, as already noted, many thought that the outer suburbs of Australian cities were badly off for the facilities to which they had been accustomed before emigration.

Although many migrant families during their first six years in Australia did secure good housing, Nightingale concluded from the evidence that many of the difficulties that migrants experienced in this regard could to some extent have been alleviated had they obtained better information, especially on all aspects of housing purchase, before they left Britain. Despite the ready availability of current Australian newspapers both at Australia House in London and at many newsagents in major British cities, the typical prospective immigrant did not take much advantage of such information sources. Nightingale doubted whether many had even tried to find out what to expect. When reinterviewed in 1967, most respondents, when asked what advice they would give to intending migrants, said that they would encourage them to bring to Australia as much as possible of their household furniture. It was a recollection that overshadowed even the difficulties of obtaining adequate housing. Many told of paying five or more times the replacement price for furniture that they had disposed of before leaving home. Although migrants were, on the whole, reasonably satisfied with their accommodation, Nightingale concluded that the British migrant would be fortunate if his permanent housing in Australia were all of the following: as large and as soundly constructed as his last home in Britain, as conveniently situated in relation to public transport, work-place and shopping centre, and as adequately serviced by sewerage and sealed roads, with kerbs and gutter. On the other hand, his Australian house will probably be newer and have a larger garden. He would also enjoy more sunshine. But a trade-off was inevitable; and satisfaction with it was an important part of the migrant's satisfaction with life in general in Australia.

Chapter 6

Coming to Terms with Australia

By their own calculations, the large majority of British migrants still living in Australia in 1967 were much better off in terms of wages and purchasing power than they had been in Britain. Furthermore, according to Nightingale, they were also much better off than their countrymen with similar skills and characteristics who had elected to stay at home. Initially, most of their savings went on building up a deposit for a dwelling and on replacing furniture and buying consumer durables that they considered necessary – either because the item in question seemed essential to life in Australia (a refrigerator, for example) or because families of the same social class who lived in suburbs were expected to own it (a car or television, for instance). But, once the durables had been acquired, and the housing deposit saved, a very high proportion of their income went on hire-purchase and mortgage repayments. Lacking substantial savings on arrival, many had been forced to acquire their consumer durables under hire-purchase arrangements and their houses through bank loans. The period of repayment was generally fairly long, depending on whether both husband and wife contributed to the family income.

Resettlement, however, touches many more aspects than economic achievement, even though the degree of satisfaction with many other aspects of Australian society was highly correlated with the degree of economic achievement. By and large, those who had done well by the end of their first six years in Australia were also the ones who showed the highest degree of satisfaction with Australian society generally. Degrees of satisfaction also changed over time. In 1960, the large number of hostel dwellers who were struggling to make ends meet expressed much lower levels of satisfaction with Australia than they expressed in 1967 when they were relocated in suburban bungalows.

Although emigrants were usually fairly well informed before departure on such key economic matters as wages, hours worked and social-security benefits, they had little prior knowledge of Australian society and so little idea of the adjustments they would have to make. Their knowledge of Australia's geography and political system was only book knowledge and even the films on Australian life that they had seen at Australia House and on the voyage out did little to prepare them for the difficulties of resettlement. I recall being seated next to a Commonwealth-nominated family during a film evening on a migrant ship in 1960. One of the films shown was about the rural wealth of New South Wales and the bright modern character of Sydney. It ended, to the accompanying strains of appropriate music, with a young Sydney surfie riding the crest of a massive wave headed for one of Sydney's northern beaches. The 40-year-old migrant, father of four, even more enthused about what he had seen than the film's producer could have ever expected, nudged his wife excitedly and proclaimed, 'Eh, luv, we'll be doin' that in a few weeks.' And he was serious, too.

For most families, the decision to emigrate had been the most important one of their married lives. Many families who decided to uproot from their council houses, sell all their possessions and emigrate with £300 to Australia, where they would be placed in Commonwealth hostels, had neither sought nor been given the kind of information and advice that could have given them a real insight into Australian society, including the general values and attitudes of Australians. Even so, the Appleyard survey confirmed that many British assisted migrants truly believed that they *were* going to a Britain in the South Seas, a land of perpetual sunshine where they would earn much higher wages than they could ever earn in Britain, where class would not be an impediment to achievement for either them or their children, where there would be no language problem and where the people were British in allegiance and friendly towards British migrants. And, while in many respects this was a fairly accurate assessment, the generalities hid many subtle nuances that would create tensions and frustrations and impede the newcomers' resettlement. How a migrant coped with these nuances depended to a large extent on his personality, especially his ability to come to terms with those aspects of the new culture that would have an important bearing upon his progress as he set about achieving the goals he had set for the new life.

Much has appeared in the press, especially in letters written by returned migrants, concerning the way they had been misled by the literature provided, and the information given, by Australia House. In the early post-war years, when a handful of officials were trying to answer enquiries by hundreds of thousands of potential emigrants, each seeking specific information relating to their personal prospects in a particular town which the official might never have visited, it was inevitable that inaccurate or incomplete information would be given. Indeed, even after the Assisted Passage Scheme had been formally launched in 1947, and it had become the practice to give every applicant a number of booklets on important aspects of Australian life, a careless comment made by the selection officer, or his guessed answer to a specific question, could be and was taken as gospel by the migrant family. The booklets were therefore revised frequently to include new information and to clarify existing information that had been misinterpreted by emigrants.

George Kiddle, an Australian official who played an important role in organising the assisted-migration scheme in London during the early post-war period, confirms that some of the original pamphlets were deficient. To Alison Ray and Allan Segal he said that, when emigrants complained about the accuracy of the information that they had been given, it was carefully scrutinised and, if necessary, altered or deleted. For example, even though Kiddle thought that the booklets on Australia's health scheme were especially helpful, because they outlined the differences between the British National Health Service and the private health-coverage system in Australia, many emigrants later complained that the differences had not been carefully articulated. Kiddle thought that alleged 'misinformation' was often misinterpretation caused by the migrant's own bias. He also confirmed the point already made that many people who decided to emigrate to Australia only listened to the good bits and did not listen to the 'crook bits'. His officials found it especially difficult to convey to migrants who had elected to work outside Australia's urban areas the nature of the environment with which they would have to cope. He recalled the occasion when a major Australian company approached his office for British migrants to work in Whyalla, South Australia. While the accommodation offered by the company was considered to be very good (three-bedroom brick houses), the town was on 'the edge of nowhere with soil that was very red and dusty', and so the houses were usually covered in dust. Though nothing could be done about this situation, it was very difficult to convey to migrants that they would have to put up with the dust, and that they might as well know the situation before they left Britain and get used to it as soon as possible after they arrived in Whyalla.

When Kiddle returned to London during the 1960s as Chief Migration Officer at Australia House, he insisted that all selection officers present the facts as fairly and as accurately as possible. His instruction to the advertising agency commissioned by the Australian government was that the country must not be oversold, although he conceded that many of the television advertisements shown during the 1960s included a lot of sand and sun. These, he argued, were designed to encourage the prospective emigrant to apply for an application form, when he would be given booklets containing accurate information on all aspects of Australian life.

What were the kinds of nuances that, individually or collectively, made resettlement a very difficult process for many migrants and, in the case of returnees, impossible? There is no doubt that the ease with which an assisted passage could be obtained after 1957 attracted many persons who were not seriously interested in hearing about the nature and the complexity of resettling in Australia. Some kept open the option of returning to Britain if things proved too difficult. Even the serious applicants tended to shrug off the possibility of problems ahead. 'We'll be all right' was a common response. In announcing Australia's first Citizenship Convention (1950), the Minister for Immigration, Harold Holt, sought the support and interest of churches, citizens' organisations and patriotic associations to assist newcomers. He also stated that the Convention was not meant for European (non-British) immigrants alone. 'The British newcomer,' he said, 'though he speaks the same language, has ties of kinship, tradition and history with Australians, and understands the general principles that form the basis of our great democracy, can also find himself lonely and misunderstood at times in his new country.'

Holt's timely warning went largely unheeded. For, while Australia, especially in the late 1940s, had strong political and economic ties with Britain, its character was only superficially British. Australia had its own culture, forged by unique historical circumstances and processes;

it was certainly not, nor could it be, a distant piece of Britain, with a similar environment, where Britsh people had merely replicated and retained British values and ways of life. The first settlers were convicts (and their military guards), who, on emancipation, injected into the new colony characteristics, attitudes and expectations that were by no means sympathetic to government authority and institutions. The physical environment was, with few exceptions, as different from Britain's as could be imagined. The first free settlers, who arrived during the early nineteenth century, probably had rather different attitudes from Britons who stayed at home. Under very difficult conditions in a harsh and trying environment they, and the emancipists, had to carve farms from the bush or establish businesses in the small new towns. Though the colonies were nurtured in a political environment largely Britsh in conception and values, Australia's colonial culture quickly developed a character which newly arrived British migrants soon discovered was very different from the culture they had left behind. As Nadel had aptly concluded, the early immigrants formed a society without a sense of mission or other-worldly justification, without native historical traditions on which to draw, and without common religious sentiments to sustain it. During the ensuing century, through gold rushes, depression and federation of the colonies into one country, an Australian culture evolved with strong egalitarian and nationalistic fervour, frequently manifest in strong criticism of the perceived exploitative role played by Britain in the nation's development. The country was British all right, but more in appearance than in the kind of complete allegiance that post-1945 Ministers of Immigaration claimed. Calwell's views in the 1930s concerning the exploitation practised by British investors in Australia, and the general worth of British migrants, probably reflected more accurately the blue-collar workers' position during the late 1940s than did the new views expressed by Calwell himself after he became Minister for Immigration.

The typical modern newcomer, though not disappointed with his higher wages, therefore soon discovered that the children of this new culture had explicit and often uncomplimentary views about his worth. The newcomer was clearly different in appearance. Some historians have suggested that the term 'Pommy', derived from 'pomegranates', was first used by waterside workers to deride the newcomers who appeared on the decks of migrant ships with red and blistered faces caused by weeks of travel in tropic seas. The newcomer also had different attitudes. Some newcomers gave the impression of feeling themselves superior; others were deliberately deferential in the belief that this would help them be accepted by the new society. They also had different values. Many a newcomer who responded to an order from the boss on his first day at work with a innocuous 'Yes, sir' was immediately labelled a 'crawler' by Australian employees and there-after subject to a great deal of criticism and abuse. The newcomer, child of another culture, was merely responding in the way expected of him in a similar situation in that culture.

For a long period of Australia's history, especially after Federation, British migrants also bore the brunt of the xenophobic attitudes of native Australians, although newcomers from non-British countries, few in number, probably suffered more indignities. After the Second World War, Australia's immigration programme became ethnically very diverse and British migrants were replaced by other nationalities as the main targets for xenophobia. Even so, the Appleyard survey revealed that few assisted migrants escaped taunts about their British origins. Those who had come with the firm intention of settling permanently in Australia, and who had used the Assisted Passage Scheme for this purpose, were generally more inclined to shrug off such comments, which invariably were good-natured and testing in intention, than were those who were less determined to resettle and had come to 'have a look at the country'. For the former, this was an inevitable part of the long process of resettlement in Australia.

A migrant's experience in coming to terms with Australian society depended largely upon where he went and with whom he came into contact. How he coped in these circumstances depended largely on his own personality. Alan Richardson, the social psychologist who worked closely with me in the 1959–67 survey of British migrants in Australia, included a number of questions in the follow-up interviews in Australia that were designed to test this theory concerning the general process of assimilation. Richardson had devised an SIA scale of assimilation, the letters representing *satisfaction*, *identification* and *acculturation*. In general terms, the three words describe stages in the journey that a migrant is required to take towards becoming an Australian. Some migrants never reach even the first stage (satisfaction) and are likely to return home; others reach the second stage (identification), but proceed no further. The satisfied migrants may live happily and comfortably in Australia but never become identified with it. Others identify with it but cannot, or will not, travel the final stage to acculturation. After years of experience in this field of research, Richardson had devised key questions the answers to which reflected just where a migrant stood in the scale of assimilation. These questions were included in the Appleyard survey in 1960 and 1967. As a result, it was possible to indicate not only the stages reached by the assisted British migrants during their first six years in Australia, but also to identify some of the problems that had prevented them from reaching higher stages.

The migrant's satisfaction with life in Australia depends upon the progress he feels he is making towards his current goals. These may be different from the goals he had expressed before emigrating. But what matters most is whether or not he is moving towards their realisation. Of great importance concerning perceived progress and the satisfaction associated with it is the more general belief that one's experiences (both positive and negative) are usually the results of one's own actions. Confidence in one's capacity to cope is also a crucial element in achieving the satisfaction stage of assimilation. To this should be added some measure of social optimism: immigrants who were more relaxed and trusting in their social relations were more likely to become satisfied than those who were not.

A number of characteristics and background experiences combined to reduce an immigrant's drive to make a go of things in Australia. Those who had reported prior to emigration that their parents were not in favour of the move were less likely to feel satisfaction during their first two or three years in Australia than those who had full parental support. If, in addition, a close bond had existed between the migrant and his/her parents left behind in Britain, each small event in Australia that worked out badly for the migrant generally provoked the parent to write disapprovingly, 'I told you so.' It did not require many experiences of this kind to undermine morale. Many migrants therefore began to doubt whether the decision to come to Australia had been a correct one. Richardson pointed out that, for married women in particular, experiences of this kind seriously undermined their desire to settle. As already noted, the wife was less likely than her husband to have been the driving force behind the decision to emigrate. Sometimes she came to Australia because that is where her husband wished to go and not because it was where she wished to go. The wife was also exposed to a greater conflict of loyalties than the husband. The follow-up interviews showed that the rate of decline in writing letters to friends and relatives in Britain was more rapid for husbands than for their wives. It was also found that significantly more wives than husbands reported experiences of homesickness. When a man was aware that his wife was dissatisfied with her life in Australia, he was more likely to say that he planned to return to Britain than if she was satisfied. Indeed, a strong desire to settle could easily be weakened when active or even passive forms of resistance to resettlement were manifested by the immigrant's wife or children.

Because the work life of a male occupies a large amount of his time and energy, as well as providing a major source of his self-esteem, failure to find suitable employment often became a serious obstacle to overall satisfaction. If a man perceived that the methods of work in Australia were different from those he had experienced in Britain, or if he felt that working conditions were worse, he would probably be dissatisfied with his situation. On a more positive note, it was shown that satisfaction with Australia generally resulted when migrants felt that their standard of living had at least been maintained or, better, had improved since coming to Australia. Because the chances of improving their standard of living were better for those who entered Australia with modest occupational and educational achievements, it is therefore not surprising to find that after seven years of residence there was a strong relationship between lower educational and occupational status and high degrees of satisfaction.

Richardson argued that, although a minimum level of overall satisfaction was the necessary foundation on which the journey towards acculturation was built, reaching identification with Australia, the second stage in the assimilation process, was the key to permanent settlement. What, then, are the conditions known to be associated with identification, or the growth of a strong attachment to Australia by British immigrants? For the husband, a shift in national identity was more likely to occur if he was younger rather than older. For the wife, the existence of parents who had approved of her move to Australia was very important. Together with these background conditions, it was close mixing with Australian-born residents that helped the migrant to feel more Australian than British. Where most of an immigrant's friends were Australian and/or he mixed more with Australians than with any other national group, there was a much greater likelihood of his becoming attached to Australia and Australians. It was when an individual felt that he was not accepted by Australians, or for some other reason, such as prolonged residence in a hostel or lack of motivation, that identification with Australia was least likely to take place. Without close contact with Australian-born residents, it was difficult for the background differences of immigrant and Australian to be forgotten or at least ignored. Contact under non-conflict conditions, where the Australian and the British migrant were equally dependent upon each other, neither having more power than the other, increased the likelihood that they would view one another as similar.

Of particular importance in reaching the final stage of acculturation was whether the migrant had taken the opportunity to immerse himself in a great number of social activities. Achievement of acculturation depended to a large extent upon length of residence, on being a very sociable person, and on having made several changes of residence and employer since arriving in Australia. It was also shown that those who had reached the acculturation stage were more likely to have been active members of organisations, clubs and societies in Britain. Furthermore, migrants who had become highly acculturated were not only socially active, but also self-reliant persons who were predisposed to change.

What proportion of migrants in the Appleyard survey had reached each of the levels in Richardson's assimilation scale? 7 per cent of men and 9 per cent of women who were still living in Australia in 1967 were classified 'dissatisfied', i.e. they had not even reached the first stage on the scale. It should be pointed out, however, that many of the sampled migrants had already returned to Britain. One may presume that many if not all of these returnees would have been in this category. The returnees' experiences are addressed in the following chapter. Richardson concluded that dissatisfied settlers were unlikely to be worse off financially than settlers at other stages of assimilation but that concern with economic security was frequently their major source of anxiety. The emotional security offered by the British system of social welfare had not been forgotten and was often contrasted with what these settlers deemed a bleak outlook if they stayed in Australia, especially if anything serious happened to affect their present earning capacity. Indeed, these anxieties had in some instances a realistic basis in experiences of hardship associated with ill health or unemployment. However, they also were often the result of a more general predisposition to anticipate calamities that might never happen. The most characteristic state of mind among the dissatisfied settlers was one of confusion. This was reflected in a wide variety of attitudes. The wife might have been critical of the quality of her accommodation or have complained about the difficulty of finding work. The husband was more likely to find fault with some aspect of his working conditions. Both were likely to believe that Australians did not accept immigrants easily and this added to their general feelings of being unsettled. Sometimes these feelings were increased by a more general sense of social isolation and this was worsened by the memory of a close-knit circle of relatives left behind in Britain.

A typical case of a dissatisfied settler was the 30-year-old sales representative who had emigrated with his 24-year-old wife and three children. When interviewed in Britain, he believed that opportunities for a better job and better accommodation would be greater in Australia than in Britain. When reinterviewed in 1961 he and his family were living in a garage on their own block of land and understandably judged that their accommodation was much less satisfactory than it had been in Britain. Nevertheless, they believed themselves to be better off in Australia and both actually said they felt more Australian than British. It was significant, however, that the interviewer reported the husband saying that, if he had known before departure what he knew then, he would never have come to Australia. However, neither he nor his wife had any plans to return to Britain; their children were happy and loved the outdoor life all year round. Life in general had become quieter for the parents and social outings were less frequent than in Britain. The atmosphere of the British pub was missed, little joy being found in the Australian hotel, which they regarded as 'quite impersonal' and like an institution. They greatly missed their relatives and friends. By 1966 they had two more sons, born in Australia, and had moved from the garage to a house on the same plot of land that they had occupied in 1961. Though they considered that their accommodation was now better than it had been in Britain, they were dissatisfied with living in the district. The wife thought it was dingy and not well cared-for, a comment that also applied to houses in her street. Neither transport nor shopping facilities were regarded as satisfactory and they had great concern about an 'undesirable element' in the neighbourhood. They reported that most mothers were said to deliver and pick up their young children from school because of fears of a prowler in the district. Both spouses said that they felt more Australian than British, although they also felt that Australians placed too much emphasis on money and what people possess. The wife's parents had stayed with them for 18 months on their way back to Britain from New Zealand. Both spouses had parents living in Britain whom they missed very much. They spoke of strong feelings of family solidarity and relations which strengthened their deep roots in Britain. However, both thought that they had made the right decision in emigrating and they intended staying permanently in Australia. Although not satisfied in general terms with Australia, their main reason for staying was that their children's future was more promising than it would be in Britain.

Satisfied settlers, as defined by Richardson, were by far the most frequent type among married migrants who were interviewed in Australia in 1967. 42 per cent of married men and 44 per cent of their wives were in this category. Compared to dissatisfied settlers, they were more likely to have shown a greater capacity to cope with their problems and a higher level of success in working constructively towards their goals. They were not only better off in a material sense since coming to Australia but they were likely to enjoy many of the less tangible qualities of their local community, including the informal pattern of social life. A practical, commonsense approach to life in Australia characterised the satisfied migrants. They did not have especially strong needs to be accepted by Australians, or to change themselves in the direction of becoming more Australian in their ways, but they did not resist making changes when change was seen as necessary for a successful adjustment. The fact that their younger children were becoming Australians and their older children were marrying into Australian families helped provide them with a sufficient sense of belonging to compensate for the absence of a strong attachment (based upon personal identification) with the new country.

Typical of the satisfied migrant was the bricklayer and his wife from Scotland who emigrated with their three school-aged children when he was 43 and his wife 38 years of age. He would have emigrated when he was demobilised from the forces in 1947, but his wife was not prepared to leave her family at that time. Though her mother was still alive when they decided to emigrate, she agreed to it for her husband's sake and for the future of their children. On their arrival in Australia they stayed in a hostel for five weeks and when interviewed in 1961 were in the process of buying their own house. When completed, she said at the time, 'it will be heaven'. Both were satisfied with the district in which they lived and reported that they were socially much more active in Australia than they had been in Scotland. They spent over 50 hours per month involved with the girls' Scottish pipe band and most of their friends were Scottish members of this organisation. Neither had felt any change in their national identification; in other words, they did not feel particularly Australian. By 1966 they were living in the house that they had been building in 1961 and regarded it as superior to the council house that they had rented in Scotland for 11 years. According to the husband, they had no prospect of ever being able to buy a house in Scotland. They liked the district in which they lived; it was close to the beach, bus and train. 'I can fit in a swim most days between morning and afternoon rounds', said the husband, who at the time was working as a postman. His wife said that they had always lived near the sea and it was so homely that they would not want to live anywhere else. They were still involved with the pipe band, around which most of their social life centred. They said their closest friends were still Scottish immigrants, although they had made contact with many nationalities, especially at work. When asked about their change in national identity, they said they were too old and settled in their ways to change much. They commented adversely on some aspects of Australian life, especially parties where men gather round the keg and wives are left together in another part of the house. This never happened in Scotland; people just talked to each other and the sexes mingled. Apart from a possible holiday in Scotland when the children were married, they intended spending the rest of their lives in Australia.

Over 20 per cent of the married men and 17 per cent of their wives had reached the identified stage of assimilation. Such families were more likely to have been predisposed to change *before* arriving in Australia; seven years after arrival they felt that they *had* changd. The husband generally believed that he was accepted by Australians and had become one of them. Being less likely to have family ties in Britain lessened the likelihood of divided loyalties. Britain was a long way away and it was no longer home. Australia was being enjoyed in the here and now and provided the ever-present context for many and varied satisfactions. Increased dependency on Australia had enhanced the sense of being Australian.

Typical of the identified settler was the underground miner aged 30 who had emigrated with his wife and daughter in 1959. On arrival in Australia they stayed in a hostel for two weeks. When reinterviewed in 1961 they thought their housing was worse than it had been in Britain, where they had left a new council house. However, they 'loved the district' in which they were living. It was, said the husband, 100 per cent better than where they had lived before. 'We were in an industrial area in England but here it is like Bournemouth or Southport.' The wife was very happy with their daughter's progress. 'She is very happy here – looks better physically – loves the beach, speaks Australian and uses slang.' The main changes in their way of life since arrival were attributed to the climate, which enabled them to get outdoors more often. The husband said that he had become much more casual. If he walked up the street in shorts back home, people would think he was crazy. 'We could never step out without a coat and tie there', he added. The wife said that, if they went for a drive on Sunday, she would spend the morning getting ready. Both of them would get 'dolled up' even though they might end up eating fish and chips. 'Here I just go as I happen to be.' She also said she loved the heat and hated the cold and this was one of the most satisfying things about Australia. Of Australians, she thought they were wonderful people to be amongst once they accept you, but you have to get to know them.

Richardson divided his acculturated settlers into quasi-acculturated and fully acculturated. 13 per cent of married men and 14 per cent of married women were of the former type. They had acquired all the material possessions they had expected before emigrating and 84 per cent of the husbands and 76 per cent of the wives hoped to spend the rest of their lives in Australia. The only major source of difficulty was in the area of social adjustment. It was not that they had no friends or no social life; their difficulties were more subtle than that. Many strongly wanted to pass as Australians and not be treated as immigrants! Some realised that their strong regional accents made it difficult for them to pass as Australians, but they would have liked to be less conspicuously different. Their children were becoming typical young Australians in speech, manner, interests and outlook, which served as a reminder of how far they had become adjusted to the country.

Fully acculturated migrants comprised the remaining 18 per cent of married men and 16 per cent of married women. They had made a very stable and happy adjustment to Australia, which had provided the kind of environment conducive to the fulfilment of their many latent potentialities. They had fitted into the social and cultural patterns of Australian life with a minimum of difficulty because the changes were in many respects a natural extension of their pre-emigration personalities. They felt Australian and in many ways they were Australian. The relaxed, easy-going social life had suited them well. Their qualities of energy and self-reliance had helped them to achieve a satisfying degree of material progress. Apart from possibly spending holidays abroad, over 95 per cent of both husbands and wives looked forward to spending the rest of their lives in Australia.

Typical of the fully acculturated settler was the Engishman aged 36 who had emigrated with his wife and one child. His decision had been made after examining prospects in other countries and coming to the conclusion that Australia provided the best opportunities. The availability of an assisted passage had certainly influenced him to choose Australia. Furthermore, the country seemed so much more open and not as built up as England. When interviewed before leaving England he had said that there was a very good chance that the family would make good in Australia if they were prepared to work. 'I know I'll not get as much money when I first get out there but I don't mind that – I'll be able to go along with a young country and not remain static as you do in England.' On arrival in Australia the family entered a Commonwealth hostel in New South Wales and were still there when interviewed in 1961. As an inducement to his wife to stay in Australia he had promised to buy a house. Though he was earning more than in England, both spouses agreed that they were worse off in Australia. He still believed that his decision to come to Australia had been correct and he wanted to stay, although his wife said that she wanted to return permanently.

When interviewed in Australia in 1966, they were living in their own house and were very satisfied with the district. The husband was now a chargehand and they owned furniture and a car. The same interviewer saw the couple in both 1961 and 1966. In her 1966 report she said, 'I well remember the couple as the wife was so dissatisfied and unhappy at the hostel. This time, I pulled up, the wife came out to the car and greeted me with the remark, "I don't think you will have forgotten me – I was such a grumbler." She assured me that she had settled down and I could see that she had. They were both very happy in Australia and had both worked hard to obtain economic security.' In retrospect,the wife felt that her main problems had been caused by hostel conditions and having to leave her young child in the care of anybody whom she could find to assist her so she could go out to work. While the husband had also disliked the hostel, he felt that the conditions had motivated him to 'work harder and to obtain our own house.' The wife said she was very satisfied with life in Australia, enjoyed the free-and-easy lifestyle and 'seldom wore more than shorts and shirt at home'. The husband described himself as more Australian than British and much better off and more satisfied than in Britain.

In assessing the information he had analysed for future policy options, Richardson placed considerable emphasis on the need for government to provide emigrants with accurate information before they left, even though the assisted British emigrant was to some extent 'buying a pig in a poke'. He could not know for certain what would happen in the future. Certain things would happen which could not rationally be attributed to the decision to emigrate. The ageing process might create more difficulties for the emigrant, but many psychological, social and economic changes would have occurred anyway. Indeed, things might have been worse had the emigrant stayed at home. Richardson also concluded that anyone considering emigration to Australia would be well advised to give serious thought to his own and his family's personal characteristics. The facts that emerge from such a self-examination are as relevant to the making of a migration decision as are the more obvious facts about conditions of life in Australia. Both types of information (i.e. about the family's personal qualities and about the planned country of settlement) should be sought and utilised but not dwelt upon indefinitely. It was also suggested that a husband or wife who did not look forward to emigration should be a cause for serious reflection by the other spouse. Although feelings may change after arrival, the likelihood of actual or implied 'I told you so' responses when things go wrong or prove difficult are greatly increased. It was vital that husband and wife should be equally enthusiastic.

Concerning the personality of a migrant, Richardson concluded that, when an individual believes that luck, chance, fate or the actions of other people are the prime determinants of rewards or punishments, he lacks a sense of personal responsibility for his fortunes. A predisposition towards cynicism, in which the individual believes that everyone is out to do him down, will inevitably meet with confirmation in Australia just as much as in Britain. Some degree of social optimism is more conducive to relaxed and enjoyable social relations in Australia as elsewhere. The absence of a strong intention to settle in Australia makes it more difficult to tolerate the 'nuances' referred to earlier in this chapter, the many irritations and frustrations of life in the new country. Ill-considered, impulsive decisions to leave Britain reduced the probability of successful settlement. The advice given by one immigrant, who said, 'Don't rush into it; talk it over with someone. First make sure that you are determined from the start to at least have a go at living in Australia and being Australian', was both wise and relevant. Without a predisposition to change, to modify one's pattern of life, stable resettlement in Australia is likely to be difficult. When one deliberately attempts to resist change, to maintain one's original national identity, one is unlikely to feel at home. Finally, because informality is a characteristic of so many aspects of Australian life, someone who values a more formal or structured lifestyle may find Australia uncongenial.

Chapter 7

Return

In seeking immigrants, Australia has traditionally sought persons prepared to be permanent settlers. Contract-labour migrants have not been encouraged, on the grounds that their presence could undermine the high standard of living achieved by Australian workers. Being uncommitted to Australian traditions, such persons might, it has been felt, be tempted to work for less than the legally binding minimum wage rates and so undermine the employment of Australians. This commitment to permanent immigration as the key to populating the sparsely settled continent has gone hand in hand with the general view that everything possible should therefore be done to minimise losses caused by migrants returning home or going to another country.

Net gains through migration therefore became an important political statistic, because they showed, in a general way, Australia's capacity to hold its immigrants. High rates of return were deplored, because they reflected adversely on the country's attractiveness and on Australians' capacity to welcome newcomers and assist them to resettle. On the other hand, little tolerance or understanding was shown for those migrants who returned. It was thought that they were not the right 'type' of persons and that Australia would be better off without them. Because the overwhelming majority of immigrants prior to 1947 were British, they became the prime target for those Australians who were offended by high return rates and by migrants who complained about Australian conditions and ways of life.

The term 'whingeing Pom' was applied to British migrants who were foolhardy enough to moan that things Australian were worse than things at home. Other European migrants, though few in number and generally from Italy, Greece and Yugoslavia, bore the main brunt of xenophobic attitudes but were none the less respected by many Australians for their capacity to work hard in difficult occupations without complaining or comparing unfavourably what they had achieved with what they had left in Europe.

Because Australia's post-war immigration programme, designed to increase population by 1 per cent per annum through immigration, had been initiated to enhance the country's defence and economic development, retaining immigrants became more important than ever. In the early post-war years, when hundreds of thousands of weary Europeans sought a new life in Australia, return by those lucky enough to have been admitted was almost unthinkable. Indeed, many of the 170,000 displaced persons who entered Australia between 1948 and 1952 could not return home; their countries were under the control of governments whose policies had caused them to become refugees.

Return by British migrants who had been lucky enough to obtain precious berths on the few migrant vessels plying to Australia between 1947 and 1950 was also unlikely. Even those who had not even reached the satisfaction stage of Richardson's assimilation scale would have been disinclined to return to the shortages, rationing and drabness that characterised Britain during the late 1940s. On 24 December 1948, Arthur Calwell reported that only 0.5 per cent of British migrants in Victoria had returned home. While rates probably increased somewhat during the early 1950s (the press certainly increased its coverage of Britons who returned because of 'intolerable conditions' experienced in Australia), return did not become a significant political issue until the mid-1950s. The timing was not accidental. As already noted, economic conditions in Britain had by then improved considerably. The worst of post-war rationing and shortages were over and emigration had become a less attractive alternative than in the late 1940s. Improved economic conditions also meant that return by dissatisfied British migrants would not be as illogical as it would have been at the end of the war. Furthermore, Britons who emigrated under the Assisted Passage Scheme during the early 1950s were probably, in many cases, less committed to permanent settlement than those who had left in the 1940s. Going out under the £10 scheme to 'take a look and see if we like it' increasingly became a more common attitude for persons whose skills, education and ages qualified them for assisted passages.

At the 1954 Citizenship Convention in Canberra, Leslie Haylen, the Opposition immigration spokesman, declared that British migrants were the 'best migrants', with no assimilation problems. Because a Briton merely 'came to this part of the Commonwealth from another part', it was disheartening to reflect on the growing numbers who were returning home. True, he declared, many came a second time, but Australia would clearly have to look more closely at the 'kind of people offering as migrants' and select those most likely to become integrated into the Australian way of life. At the 1956 Convention, the executive director of Australia's Building Industry Congress (Stewart Fraser), reported that, while 2 per cent of non-British migrants returned to Europe, the percentage for British migrants had increased to 6. Most returned, he said, for personal reasons, especially homesickness, but many of them re-emigrated to Australia at their own expense after realising, from renewed contact with the old country, 'that this young country really has something which their homeland cannot provide'.

By 1957, however, rates of return by British migrants were large enough to spark a major political storm in what had hitherto been an area in which the two main parties had no disagreement. The Citizenship Convention heard Gough Whitlam declare not only that the British proportion of Australia's migrant intake was now much lower than had been reported by the government, but that return rates had increased mainly because of inadequate government policies concerning housing and social security. 'What is very alarming', declared Whitlam, 'is that of the people who go back to the countries of Europe from Australia . . . more go back to Britain than to other countries.' Of the 29,000 people who had left Australia in 1956, said Whitlam, 19,000 went back to Britain.

Whitlam's criticism led officials and academics to define and assess the 'rate of return' more carefully, and especially to explore the reasons why migrants were leaving Australia. Borrie's paper at the next Convention (1958) provided some of the answers. Because movement between Britain and Australia (and other Commonwealth countries) had been much freer from restrictions and regulations than movement between Australia and non-Commonwealth countries, it was easier for a migrant to return home if he had come from Britain than if he had come from a country outside the Commonwealth. He calculated that, although the British proportion of permanent arrivals in Australia was 47 per cent, the *net* permanent gain was only 34 per cent. His

97

calculation was something of a bombshell in the normally sedate Convention, and sparked much debate on why the difference was so large and what could be done to reduce it. Borrie, however, foreshadowed the reaction by writing that, before judgement was passed, a great deal more information should be obtained on the content of the return flow: for example, on how many returnees were pre-war immigrants and how many were recent arrivals, and whether the outflow of persons of British nationality included some 'disgruntled Australians'! Furthermore, he wrote, a high circular flow was inevitable given the close relations and cultural links between the two countries. The Convention needed to know more about the composition of the return flow, and how many former British immigrants had left because they were disgruntled, and why they had become disgruntled.

The Australian government responded to these questions by commissioning research into the settlement of British migrants in Australia. Officials initially proposed that answers to the questions raised by Borrie could be obtained by interviewing returnees as they stepped aboard vessels at Australian ports for the journey back to Britain. But wiser heads argued that such interviews would not explain all aspects of the returnee problem. A major project was therefore launched by the Australian National University which was based on the proposition that the returnee problem could only be understood by comparing the experiences of returnees with those of migrants who stayed in Australia. It was therefore decided to interview a sample of emigrants before they left Britain and follow them up in Australia. Returnees could then be compared with stayers on the basis of characteristics, attitudes and expectations before emigrating and on the basis of their experiences in Australia. The research project became known as the Appleyard survey.

By the end of 1957, however, well before the Appleyard survey could provide results, the grievances of British migrants in Commonwealth hostels were being reported almost daily in both the local and British press. While the Australian government agreed that it was right to begin field research in Britain before persons emigrated to Australia, it also sought as much immediate information as was available on all aspects of contemporary return flows. Thus, in addition to directing the main survey, I was asked to assess the extent and composition of current return flows. I visited Britain and made contact with the Ministry of Pensions office in Newcastle upon Tyne, where, at my request, a 20 per cent sample was taken of application forms by persons who had re-registered for social security on return from Australia. Letters were sent by the Ministry to the families so sampled requesting them to contact me with a view to being interviewed about their experiences in Australia. 42 per cent responded. Interviews conducted with them in their homes explored their general background, preparation for emigration to Australia, experiences there, and experiences in Britain upon return. The information collected during those interviews indicated two main clusters of returnees: those who had been in Australia for periods of two to four years and those who had been there for six or more years. The first cluster contained a large proportion of British assisted migrants who had fulfilled their obligation to the Australian government to stay for two years or else repay the cost of their outward passages. All returnees had clearly been much better off in Australia than they had been in Britain before emigrating. The average hourly earnings of both male and female workers in the first jobs in Australia respectively, were, 50 and 42 per cent higher than their average daily earnings in their last jobs in Britain before they emigrated. Upon return to Britain, male and female workers' average hourly earnings were, respectively, 25 and 21 per cent lower than their earnings in their last jobs in Australia. Although less than half the married respondents had transferred less than £200 to Australia, while there they had accumulated substantially more capital than they had been able to save in Britain before emigration. Indeed, their annual rate of capital accumulation was almost ten times higher in Australia than it had been in Britain. They had also acquired almost all the main consumer durables while in Australia: 61 per cent of those who had not owned a car in Britain, 42 per cent of those who had not owned a washing machine, and 45 per cent of those who had not owned a refrigerator purchased these durables while in Australia.

In such circumstances, one may question the economic rationality of their decisions to return. The reasons given for return were extremely varied. Former assisted respondents, mainly those who had been in Australia for a little over two years, gave 'wife's homesickness' as the main reason why they had come back. Other important reasons were either death or illness of a relative. Only a minority indicated that Australian employment and housing conditions had been the main reasons for their return. While it is not possible to identify the position of any of these persons on Richardson's assimilation scale, it is clear that many were so dissatisfied with their situation in Australia that they saw return as the only viable option. Having made their decision to return, and some took the decisions within months of arrival, the families then concentrated on saving for their return passage. During this period their dislike of things Australian increased, as did their recollections of all the good things about life in Britain.

On my way to Britain by ship, I had met many returning British migrants who complained bitterly about life in Australia. Unfortunate personal experiences and anti-British attitudes of Australians were given as the main reasons why they had decided to return. However, the experiences related by the migrants in the Ministry of Pensions sample differed so greatly from what I had heard on the voyage to Britain that I made arrangements for those people I had seen on the ship to be reinterviewed in Britain. It transpired that, once they were back home, their stories of their experiences in Australia, and their recollections of that country, had changed enormously. In several instances, information given me by families aboard the returning migrant ship bore no relation whatever to the information they gave an independent interviewer in Britain a few months later. In one such case, the returnee told me that he had lived in a one-bedroom flat with his wife and child in central Melbourne, that he had been unemployed for half the two-year period he had been in Australia, that his son had suffered an accident and that his wife had contracted a disease. All these things combined to decide him to return to Britain. When seen in Briain some months later, he told an interviewer, who did not identify herself with my project, that he had lived in a three-bedroom brick house in a Melbourne suburb, that his son had been happy at school, and that his only reason for returning was that his wife had wanted to come back for a long holiday to see her parents.

I concluded that the return voyage was an extremely important part of the return experience. Many respondents had to face friends and relatives who had only recently bade them farewell and wished them success in the new land. To return so soon after could have been construed as an admission of failure. The returnees therefore had to devise a 'story' of life in Australia so compelling that it could be seen that return was their only option.

Once resettled in Britain, respondents to the Ministry of Pensions survey clearly had second thoughts about the correctness of their decisions. Recollection of much better economic circumstances and the warmer climate in Australia had made many of them regret their decisions to return to Britain. In fact, when asked whether they had any plans to return to Australia, nearly 68 per cent said 'yes' and a further 8 per cent were undecided. Many had already made enquiries about new assisted passages.

What had happened to make them change their minds within six months of return? 'Home' is a complex concept of memories and experiences where, wrote James Thurber, a man's relationship with six or eight persons and two or three buildings is of greater importance than what goes on in the nation or in the universe. The immigrant in Australia, no matter how easily or rapidly he may adjust to his new environment, often remembers the buildings he knew and relationships he used to have. As already noted, nearly 40 per cent of the former assisted families in the Ministry of Pensions survey stated that 'wife's homesickness' was the main reason why they returned to Britain. Although returnees gave long and introspective replies to questions about their reactions to life in Britain since their return, three general factors emerged as having an important bearing on their attempts to readjust to British society.

The first related to physical environment. Many workers who returned to the industrial cities of Britain (the source of most of Australia's assisted British migrants) typically had negative reactions to their physical environment. A lorry driver's reply was typical: 'I thought it was bloody awful. I always thought London was a great place. The sight of Tilbury shocked me. If it wasn't for my wife I'd be back [to Australia] tomorrow.' An electrician's wife, who returned to her parents' home in a terraced building in Preston, Lancashire, reflected, 'Hum-drum. It's hard to settle down despite a good summer. Awful to come back to a street like this; people have been here for generations – just hum-drum.' Others who returned to industrial cities also complained that they were dirty, cold and miserable, rather dull and very cramped, although those who returned to semi-detached houses and residential areas seldom complained about the physical environment. All respondents, when asked what aspect of life in Australia they found most satisfying, replied that its outdoor life and climate and the friendliness of Australians headed the list.

Family relations were the second important aspect of readjustment. In only a few cases was homecoming the experience which returnees had hoped it would be. Obsessed by their determination to return to

Britain, they had painted a mental picture of their home and environment which hardly resembled reality, and so were disappointed. Only a minority implied that everything was as they had expected. Respondents were usually bewildered by their homecoming for they, not home, had changed. With writers as various as Marcel Proust and Thomas Wolfe they had discovered that you can't go home again. Contact with an environment and culture so different from Britain's had unobtrusively affected their outlook and value patterns. They now saw home through new eyes, and the first excitement of meeting family and friends was often followed by a period of sobering readjustment. While most of the migrants had initially planned to return to Britain permanently, many changed their views and said that they had come back only for a long holiday. Those who were genuine long-holiday-makers could stand aloof and muse at the situation; those who had decided to return permanently had to try to adjust to what was really a new situation. And, while they expected that their more insensitive relatives and friends would assess their return as an admission of failure, they also hoped to be remembered and welcomed and take up relationships where they had left them. But, predictably, many returnees complained that their old friends seemed cool, that they hadn't been missed at all and that the return had been nowhere near as exciting as the farewell. Then, inevitably, old friends had made new friends and were often not as ready to resume old friendships as the returnees had hoped they would be. One spoke for many when he said, 'I went back to the pub I used to visit and couldn't find a soul I knew.' How often he must have thought about his return to the old pub when he was in Australia!

The survey also revealed that the returnees quickly became intolerant of the way things were done in the old country. A single schoolteacher admitted that she was now more intolerant of her family than she remembered being before she went to Australia. 'I know I've changed. They haven't. With my friends at work this doesn't matter because these friendships are more flexible and are on a less emotional basis.' Some of the conflict with relatives was probably exacerbated by the returnee's understandable tendency to compare things in Britain with 'the way we did it in Australia', and the less sophisticated could easily have degenerated into bores. Finally, there was conflict caused by parents who had induced their children to return by writing of illness in the family. In some cases, their exaggeration of minor ailments formed the basis of argument as well as a convenient peg upon which the returnees could hang their disappointment with home and their determination to return to Australia.

The third general aspect of the returnees' situation related to economic conditions. Nearly all the former assisted respondents had earned much higher incomes in Australia. On re-entering the workforce in Britain, lower income with its lower purchasing power was very hard to accept. 'I'm working harder and longer for half the Australian pay', said one. 'You can't make the same money in England', said another. However, by working eight to ten hours longer in Britain, several returnees had been able to earn fairly similar weekly wages.

Although the Ministry of Pensions survey offered considerable insights into the resettlement of returnees, it did not clarify the significant problems associated with measuring the rate of return. Aside from inadequate statistical data, the concept is based upon the returnees' expectations, and these, of course, can and do change. Thus, persons who left Australia with the firm intention of resettling permanently in Britain would be counted as returnees in the statistics, even though, as was often the case, they soon changed their minds and declared that they had only come back for a long holiday and would return to Australia fairly soon. One of the advantages of the Appleyard longitudinal survey, i.e. the main survey reported in this book, is that by following migrants over a number of years it was able to identify the number of return visits that they made to the homeland and also identify their reasons for making those visits.

The Appleyard survey, based upon interviews with migrants before they emigrated and on two occasions during their first six years in Australia, also provided many insights into the decision-making processes of returnees. During the seven-year period of the study, 71 per cent of the interviewed migrants remained in Australia as settlers and 29 per cent returned to Britain. This 29 per cent comprised 15 per cent (about half) who were still there in 1966; 11 per cent who re-emigrated to Australia; and 3 per cent who had moved on to New Zealand. Thus, for the seven-year period under discussion, the net loss to Australia from the entire sample was 18 per cent. Rate of loss varied according to the sex and the marital status of immigrants on first arrival in Australia. The order from lowest to highest loss was as follows: single women who married after arrival in Australia, 13 per cent; single men who married after arrival in Australia, 15 per cent; couples who were married before arrival in Australia, 18 per cent; men who remained single, 20 per cent; and women who remained single, 37 per cent. The survey showed that the departers were less assimilated in 1961, in terms of the Richardson scale, than were those who became settlers. They were less satisfied and less likely to express a desire to settle permanently in Australia. It was especially interesting to discover that the average period that an immigrant family stayed in Australia before returning to the United Kingdom was two years and nine months. The decision for most had been made within the first year of their arrival in Australia, and they spent the remaining one to two years saving for their return passages. An immigrant who returned or moved on to another country was clearly still searching for an environment that would provide a greater degree of satisfaction for his particular combination of needs, interests and values. An immigrant who returned directly to his homeland was clearly less likely to consider searching for an environment closer to his ideal, but had more often limited his choice to either Britain or Australia.

Returnees in the Appleyard survey may be conveniently classified as either permanent returnees or potential re-emigrants. Already in 1961, before many of the returnees had yet departed from Australia, the two sub-types had different opinions about Australia. More of those who were to become permanent returnees made unfavourable comparisons between their standard of living as it was in Australia with what it had been in Britain. Only 42 per cent of permanent returnee husbands and 50 per cent of their wives reported that the standard of living was the same as or better than it had been in Britain. The comparable figures for potential re-emigrants were 56 per cent for husbands and 67 per cent for wives. Persons who remained single in Australia were more likely to return to Britain than those who married while there. The single person tended to treat the experience as a long holiday without commitment to settlement. For families, however, the decision was not so simple. It is interesting to note that migrants who arrived in Australia with the largest amounts of capital were more likely to return than those who arrived with small amounts. On the other hand, Commonwealth nominees who had been resident in hostels during at least a part of their stay in Australia were more likely to think about returning than personal nominees who had lived initially with close

Nissen huts, Nunawading Hostel.

Children's playground, Bonegilla Reception Centre. (Photographs: Australian Dept. of Immigration, Canberra.)

Serving meals in the dining room at Fairy Meadow Hostel.

Washroom facilities, Bonegilla Reception Centre. (Photograph: Australian Dept. of Immigration, Canberra.)

Mr and Mrs John O'Connor built their first home in Australia with their bare hands.

Arthur Calwell, former Minister for Immigration, addressing the first Citizenship Convention. (Canberra, 1950.) (Photographs: Australian Dept. of Immigration, Canberra.)

Australia's one millionth post-war migrant, Mrs Barbara Porritt lived in this pre-cut house which had been shipped from England.

Mr and Mrs Porritt (centre) are welcomed to Australia by Mr (and Mrs) Harold Holt, Minister for Immigration. (Photographs: Australian Dept. of Immigration, Canberra.)

Alan Brooks and his wife Debra, return to Britain after emigrating to Australia for just 72 hours. The Brooks complained they could not find jobs in Australia (31 May, 1978). (Photograph: Press Association.)

Poms in the sun. (Photograph: Australian Dept. of Immigration, Canberra.)

Like so many immigrants, the first leg of the Throssel family's journey to Australia was by train from their home in Hull. (Taken from the Granada Television documentary, *This England: Take It or Leave It*, 1965.)

Steven Throssel, 23 years later, has settled near Perth in Western Australia. He now works as a seaman at the BP Oil Refinery at Kwinana. (Photo by Alison Ray, 1987.)

Above Kathy Dolan left behind her family in Stocksbridge, Yorkshire, to start a new life in Australia. Kathy is now a successful Melbourne businesswoman. (Taken from the Granada Television documentary, *This England: Take It or Leave It*, 1965.)

Left Joe and Mary Aspinall left Leigh in Lancashire with their five children in 1965. They are now retired and live in a Perth suburb. Joe worked for many years in the Western Australia mining industry. (Photo by Alison Ray, 1987.)

Josie and David Hall with their son Karl on their way to Australia. David had secured a job as a geologist in the remote Western Australia goldfields. (Taken from the Graňada Television documentary, *This England: Take It or Leave It*, 1965.)

David and Josie Hall now live near Devonport in Tasmania. David is Regional Exploration Manager for a large mining company, while Josie runs a commercial catering business. (Photo by Alison Ray, 1987.)

friends or relatives. This was especially true of migrants who had been in hostels for long periods.

The 1966 survey covered settlers who had remained in Australia as well as migrants who had returned to Britain. Although the interviews conducted with returnees in Britain separated permanent returnees from potential re-emigrants, some migrants had already re-emigrated to Australia a second time. Permanent returnees were more likely than potential re-emigrants to have been motivated by failure to fulfil their material expectations of Australia. For example, one husband said he was working six or seven days a week, and if there was any illness in the family he felt he would never get on his feet again. His wife declared that there was no future for them in Australia, because her husband had to work such long hours to make a living. Another husband said that he could not see how he could ever accumulate enough capital for a deposit on a dwelling. He was never able to move from a Commonwealth hostel during his stay in Australia and a large proportion of his earnings was spent on board. He felt friendless and had no one to whom he could turn for advice or in whom he could confide. His wife said that she could see herself working full time until she was 65 and still not achieve half of what she thought the family could achieve in Britain. Another husband blamed the uncertainty of employment; he never felt secure and could not settle down because he had no ties or roots. His wife said that she was especially homesick at Christmas, that schooling was poor, and that she did not believe that their children would obtain good jobs once they had left school.

The sense of being unsettled and insecure in Australia was much less apparent among returnees who had become potential re-emigrants. More important in motivating the potential re-emigrant were unanticipated social and emotional problems created by their being in Australia. For example, one husband said his mother had kept writing to say how lonely she was, which made him feel guilty. His wife said that her mother-in-law made life unbearable with her 'moaning letters'. Another husband said he got so fed up with the hostel and his wife was so miserable that he finally decided that she would be better off back in Britain. The wife agreed that hostel life had got her down and that when her sister's baby was born in Britain she decided to return. Thus more of the permanent-returnee couples gave reasons associated with some specific dissatisfaction of a material kind (for instance, work, economic conditions, housing or social services) than did potential re-emigrants, who appear to have been less economically secure or desperately homesick. They returned to Britain either because family or other ties obliged them to do so or because of the physical/emotional health of husband or wife.

When reinterviewed in 1966 in Britain, many returnees had been back for several years. Those who intended to stay permanently in Britain had by this time made satisfactory adjustments. They preferred to stay where they were rather than move anywhere else. 70 per cent reported having achieved their long-term housing plans, compared with an equal percentage of their compatriots who had become settlers in Australia. Those who had left Australia because of social and family reasons in Britain were now more likely to be interested in the possibility of re-emigrating. Only 56 per cent of that group reported that they had achieved their long-term housing plans.

The permanent returnees expressed delight at being back in Britain. One husband said it was 'wonderful to be back among familiar people and circumstances' and his wife said she felt so good because everything was so homely, whereas out in Australia there were houses not homes. Everything in Britain was clean and fresh after the dust, dirt and sand out there. Another husband said he had settled down well since returning and felt more secure, and his wife declared that Britain was the best country in the world and that you have to go to another country to appreciate your own. A third commented that economic conditions in Britain were improving every year. He said that he now appreciated the gentleness of Britain and that Australia was a very hard country. His wife responded that she felt safe and really contented.

On the other hand, potential re-emigrants were less satisfied with their situations. One husband complained that nothing had changed in Britain; that climate, working conditions and pay were worse than in Australia. His wife said that the family was in a rut and almost immediately upon return made her decision to return to Australia. Another husband said that everything he saw in Britain was dirty, that he and his wife weren't excited for a single minute after they had arrived. This was confirmed by his wife, who said everything looked so crowded and dull and drab. A third family were very unsettled because they had left their children in Australia, where they (the parents) had found it difficult to make friends. They missed their children very much and this had coloured their views about Britain and quickened their decision to return to Australia as soon as possible.

Predictably, those who had actually re-emigrated to Australia were glad to be back. Typical of these families was one husband that complained about horrible living accommodation and low wages in Britain, that the number of coloured people was larger than ever, and that the general attitude was that you lived for today with no eye to the future. His wife referred to unpleasant attitudes of take-it-or-leave-it and everyone content with what they had. Another husband said that the family weren't wanted back in Britain, that people were not interested in them and that they didn't even want to see their photographs! This was confirmed by his wife. Yet another husband complained bitterly about the climate and that people's attitudes seemed to have changed, although after six months he realised that it was his own outlook and attitude that had changed.

To summarise, permanent returnees had emigrated to Australia with the hope of improving their standard of living. After 18 months in Australia they were likely to describe themselves as relatively well satisfied, and, although they persisted in their attempts to achieve economic and social security, sometimes for another year or more, in the end they decided to cut their losses and return home. They were not likely to be effective social mixers and in fact had made little contact with Australians during their stay. Nostalgia for Britain became very strong and attachment to Australia very weak. Back in Britain the economic security provided by the welfare state and the social and emotional security provided by their close-knit extended family confirmed the correctness of their decisions. Thus, when re-interviewed in Britain after several years' residence they expressed great satisfaction at being back and had no wish to emigrate anywhere ever again.

Potential re-emigrants were likely to have been relatively well satisfied with the progress they had made after 18 months' residence in Australia. Although they were less satisfied than migrants who did not return to Britain, they *had* made Australian friends and had formed some degree of attachment to the new country. Their decision to return to Britain was often taken with reluctance, but ill health, or more often family pressure or obligations in Britain, had forced them to return. After arrival, the majority developed feelings of homesickness for Australia. Britain clearly had disappointed them. Compared with Australia it often appeared colder, dirtier, smaller and generally more depressing than they had expected. They did not resettle easily but could not afford to fulfil their wish to re-emigrate. On the whole, they were more likely to be worse off in material terms than those who had stayed in Australia.

Returnees who actually re-emigrated to Australia were considerably better off financially than any other returnees and considerably better off than those who had not returned. Their decision to return to Britain was prompted by a desire to see their families once again and was often acknowledged as only a holiday visit. Many of them had actually bought return tickets before they left Australia and the majority expected to return there eventually. However, the reception they received from friends and relations did not stimulate a desire to stay permanently. For the most part, they found that few people were interested in their migration experiences. This, coupled with the material discomforts of cold and wet weather, led the majority to say that they were pleased to be back in Australia.

Chapter 8

The Migrants Speak: Granada's Quartet

In 1965, Granada produced a television documentary entitled *This England: Take It or Leave It*. Three young British families and one single girl who had decided to emigrate to Australia were interviewed in their homes, workplaces and on the migrant trains from London to the docks where they joined different vessels for Australia. Like the Britons in the Appleyard survey six years earlier, they were asked why they had decided to emigrate and what they hoped to achieve in Australia. Although economic conditions in Britain had improved considerably during those six years, Australia's economy was in its post-war golden era, providing employment for thousands of immigrants from Europe. British assisted migrants were especially in demand during the 1960s. They filled skilled and semi-skilled jobs in the industrial sectors, where their trade qualifications were readily accepted, and jobs in those service sectors where an ability to speak English was a necessary qualification. Migrants from southern European countries, on the other hand, filled unskilled jobs in the growing industrial districts around Melbourne and Sydney.

Granada's researchers visited Australia in 1966 and reinterviewed the three couples and the single girl to find out what they had already achieved, whether the expectations they had expressed before emigrating had been fulfilled and the difficulties they had experienced during their first six months. Although the procedure adopted by Granada for this follow-up survey was similar to the procedure adopted in the Appleyard survey, a salient difference was the shorter period that

Granada's migrants had been in Australia – six months compared with about 21 for the Appleyard sample.

In 1987, twenty-one years later, Granada set out to discover what had happened to the quartet. Under the direction of Allan Segal, interviews were conducted with the same migrants, all of whom were still living in Australia. This aspect of the Granada project was especially important, because, unlike the Appleyard survey, which last saw the sampled migrants six years after they reached Australia, Granada's programme saw them at a time when children and babies who had left England in 1965 were now 20 or more years old. While the children knew little or nothing about Britain, their parents, the original migrants, were able to recall very clearly the difficulties and the consequences of their original decisions to emigrate to Australia. Their long, often introspective, replies to questions posed by Alison Ray and Allan Segal provided many insights into the assimilation process.

*　　　*　　　*

Steve and Pat Throssel lived in Hull, Yorkshire, where he worked as a railway labourer and earned £10 a week. Pat worked as a machinist in a shoe factory and with overtime earned twice as much as her husband. Steve's job was to follow railway carriages along the tracks in shunting yards and control their speed by manipulating brakes with a specially designed wooden stick. They lived in a terraced house near the centre of Hull. It had two storeys with three bedrooms up top and a living room and kitchen down below. When interviewed in 1965, Steve expressed negative views about his position and prospects in England and very positive hopes concerning better prospects in Australia. He expected that the children would be better off in Australia, where, unlike in Britain, there was a good education system in which those who showed promise were encouraged to achieve. He also believed that housing in Australia would be much better and more comfortable than his terrace-type dwelling in Hull. He was especially looking forward to having a much larger plot of land, where his children could play and not have to run on the street. The higher wages that he had been told were paid in Australia would be sufficient for the family's needs. His wife would therefore not have to work to make ends meet as they were doing in Hull. 'Here', he said 'she's earning more money than what I am – up to £23 a week while I get £11. That's not good – it's ridiculous.'

110

Steve was flexible about the kind of employment he would accept in Australia, but hoped to get into the building trade. He had been thinking about emigrating for several years, but the prospect of redundancy finally decided him to make a new start elsewhere. The Assisted Passage Scheme had attracted him to Australia, where he expected to achieve a great deal more than he was achieving in Britain. He also expected that his two small children would have much better long-term prospects in Australia.

Pat was not as enthusiastic about the venture as was Steve. When interviewed a few weeks before they left for Australia, she expressed concern about her mother's feelings, especially because her mother had become very attached to the children, whom she cared for while Pat was at work. 'You can tell she's gone quiet this last week – I don't talk about it much and she seems to be always wanting the bairns with her. We see her taking last glimpses of all the photographs of us together and putting them in frames and just generally hanging around – you know.'

After an uneventful voyage, the Throssels disembarked at Fremantle. First impressions were not good. Although much had been said about Australia's sunshine, it was pouring with rain when they reached port and all Steve could see from shipside was 'a load of sand and I thought, "Oh Christ, what have we come to?"' Pat felt much the same, and when interviewed in Western Australia the following year said that after a month in Australia the novelty had worn off and she realised that she was 'stuck here and if anything goes wrong, the slightest thing, I'd start thinking about home'. However, they were determined to stay, hoping that things would improve.

When Steve became depressed, he would compare the snow and ice of northern England with the sun and sand of Fremantle. He also realised that he would be foolish to make a hasty decision and was determined to give the venture a fair go. However, his feelings vacillated daily; one day he was all for staying; the next he was 'as bad as ever again'. Receiving letters from home was a particularly distressing experience. In England he had thought that everything would be much the same in Australia except that he would be better off and there would be more sunshine and better weather. 'But, it's not like that at all. *You* really have to change.'

Pat too made a firm decision to give Australia a fair chance. She looked at all the unhappy English migrants planning to go home and realised that she was becoming like them, thinking all the time that she must get home. They spent only a week in a hostel before obtaining a flat in Fremantle. However, they resented paying the high rent and so decided to purchase a house. The estate agent took them to areas where three-bedroom brick bungalows were being built on quarter-acre plots of land. When the agent told him that the houses would cost about £3000 Steve was astounded, because he had been told by Australia House in London that a house in Western Australia could be purchased for much less and on payment of £150 deposit. However, he was able to borrow £3000 from his bank, something he believed would not have been possible in England for a man of his social class.

Although Steve had been sponsored by the Western Australian Government Railways, he had been told on the outward voyage by another migrant family that he would not have to honour the obligation if he thought he could do better elsewhere. He had expected work as a shunter on the railways, but became rather alarmed by the dangerous procedures adopted by the Western Australian Railways and so decided to find a better job.

A friend found him a job as a plasterer's labourer, but the wet lime used by the company burnt his hands and thereafter he had to wear gloves. On his way to his next job, in a polythene factory, located on the fringes of an industrial area, he sought directions from a worker in another factory who told him that his company was also looking for workers. As the wages they offered were almost double those offered for the job to which he was going, Steve accepted the offer. Jobs were plentiful in Western Australia at that time, and employers were quite desperate for workers.

When interviewed in 1966, Steve had already formed strong opinions about Australian society. He thought that all Australians were more or less the same, that nobody classed himself higher than anyone else, because the difference in wages was not great. In England, he said, the boss had a big flashy car and you had only a bicycle. But in Australia the boss has a big flashy car and you may have one even newer than his. The boss goes home to his big house and you go home to your big house, whereas in England he goes home to his big mansion and you go back to your terraced house. Nor was he disappointed with the climate. 'When you go to work', he said, 'it's sunshine all the way, whereas in England you get up in the morning, light three fires and

112

then put on all your gear, including three overcoats and four pairs of socks, and sit down to breakfast before braving the outdoors.'

Pat thought it was too early to predict whether or not she would stay or return to England. There were times when she wished she could go home, but she still really intended 'giving it a try' because she had observed that once newcomers settled into a really good community many of their problems of homesickness disappeared. The first four months were really critical. She knew a person who came to Australia with dreams of making a fortune but stayed for only a month.

Although Steve had been a member of the British Seamen's Union in Hull, he had left the merchant navy to work ashore as a labourer in the railways. His British Seamen's Union's ticket stood him in good stead in Australia. On making enquiries with the Australian Department of Transport for employment in the Australian merchant navy, he was told that the waiting list was very long and that he should seek other employment. Seven years later he received a telegram from the Department inviting him for a job interview. Having already achieved leading-hand status with an industrial painting firm, Steve was reluctant to accept the offer, but in retrospect is pleased that he did. When interviewed by Alison Ray and Allan Segal in 1987, he was still working as a deckhand on a tugboat servicing the BP Oil Refinery at Kwinana. Although the weather was frequently turbulent in winter, on average the worst weather was the norm on the Humber whence he came.

Steve is a very relaxed, friendly person who takes no offence at the good natured banter he receives from Australians with whom he works. Though he is frequently called a Pommy bastard, it does not upset him because he feels that it is usually used as a term of endearment. He always laughs off such remarks and never takes offence. After Pat found employment, her bouts of homesickness were replaced by enthusiasm equal to Steve's. Initially, however, she found it very difficult to cope with the hot weather, which she used as an excuse in the first few months to try and persuade Steve to take her back to England.

After buying the house they had seen with the estate agent in 1966, the Throssells then changed house many times – an estimated seven. Three of the homes in the seven or eight moves they made during 20 years were new. The satisfactory aspect of their mobility was that each acquisition represents an improvement in their standard of living. When asked by Allan Segal whether he thought he would have had the kind of confidence necessary to make such capital gains had he remained in England, Steve, supported strongly by Pat, firmly replied 'no', although being a home-owner in England before emigrating had given him the confidence to be both mobile and enterprising in Australia.

At the 1987 interview, Pat ruminated about her bouts of homesickness. She would advise British wives not to make close contact with other British wives in similar situations. Complainers made her depressed; she found herself agreeing with them immediately, not fighting them. Now she argues with people who express similar critical views and tells them to give the country a chance before reaching negative conclusions. During the first few months in Australia she lived in the Italian district of Fremantle, where she met many new Australians. Although she tried to make contact with the non-English speaking Italian wives, it was the lack of contact with Australians that was a main reason why her homesickness was so prolonged.

Pat's homesickness eventually became so serious that Steve decided to take her back to England. In those days (1966), you had to book about 12 months in advance, and by the time they were due to leave she had become much better adapted to Australian society, had made many Australian friends and was reluctant to leave. 'When I walked up the gangplank, I knew I had made the wrong decision. In fact, during the last month I was thinking that we shouldn't be doing what we had decided to do. It was a wrong move.'

The four years they stayed in England was described by the Throssels as quite happy. But, although they visited many parts of England, they knew that their future lay in Australia. The decision to emigrate a second time was confirmed after meeting friends in similar circumstances. The small business they had bought in England had to be sold at a loss, but it was a small price to pay for the experience of discovering their identity. On applying to Australia House for second assisted passages, they were told by an official that returnees were generally encouraged to re-emigrate because they knew what to expect in Australia and would therefore be unlikely to return again. Although neither Pat nor Steve were granted second assisted passages, their children were on the grounds that they had been brought back to England by their parents.

Steve's job satisfaction was very high. He was pleased to be back in Australia doing the kind of work he had always wanted to do. He has

114

had no difficulty communicating with Australians. As he had said in 1966, he liked their attitude, the absence of class distinctions, and the fact that you didn't have to prove anything. 'It's not class distinction; it's just we're all the same.' Both Pat and Steve said they felt the children were also much better off, having been better educated than they would have been had they remained in England. The measure of the Throssels' satisfaction with Australia was conveyed by their answer to a question whether, if offered a trip back to England to live permanently, they would take it. Both answered a firm 'no'. Steve thought that they had been very successful in Australia because they were outgoing adventurous people who wanted to do things for themselves, and Australia was the very place where this kind of attitude was encouraged.

*   *   *

Kathy Dolan, a pretty young girl in her early twenties, came from Stocksbridge in the north of England, where she worked as a clerk. She could see no future in Stocksbridge and was determined to seek her destiny elsewhere, an objective not shared by her parents, who tried strongly to dissuade her from emigrating to Australia under the Assisted Passage Scheme. But Kathy was in a rut. She claimed that she, like her parents, was doing the same things over and over again. Friends in Australia had told her it was all so different out there. In Britain people just seemed to go along doing the same things, whereas in Australia they have their own ideas and fulfil them in ways they believe are satisfying and fulfilling.

Stocksbridge was not a pleasant town; its skyline was dominated by smoke stacks, and in winter it was dull and depressing. Although Kathy looked upon emigration to Australia as an adventure, she did not believe that she would remain there for the rest of her life. During the farewell party at her office, she was told how much they appreciated her work and were certain that she would make 'a success of your life there . . . and would not let the good name of England and Yorkshire down'. The final break from her family was a sad but not traumatic event. She made her way alone to the migrant ship, where she met other girls of her own age. On arrival in Sydney, they shared a flat.

When interviewed in Sydney in 1966, Kathy had experienced no difficulties in settling into the Australian society. She soon obtained a job similar to the one she had had in Stocksbridge, and earned £17 a week. Rent for the flat she had acquired was 10 guineas a week, but this and the cost of food and rent on a television were shared by all the girls. Kathy told the interviewer that she felt more independent in Australia. Back home she had to think about, and sometimes fall back upon, her family if anything went wrong. In Australia she was on her own and had to solve her own problems. Her adaptation had been especially rapid. She never thought much about England; in fact, it seemed as if she'd never lived there. On her arrival in Australia she said to herself, 'Well, Kathleen, you're here and you're going to make the best of it.' Looking back to her decision to leave Stocksbridge, she said that she had come to the conclusion that she had really done nothing with her life and that emigration would provide her the opportunity to better herself. She had found that Australia was a country for young people and wished that more young English people would come and see for themselves what they were missing. The thing that impressed her most about Australians was their friendliness; she had never been taunted about being a Pommy. The only time she really thought about England was when she received letters from home. She was becoming more like an Australian and was content to remain in Sydney and was not particularly interested in what was happening outside the country.

When Alison Ray saw Kathy Dolan in Melbourne in November 1987, her identification with Australia was almost complete. She talked about having noticed a real change in the country and the people since her arrival 20 years before. She strongly disagreed with the suggestion that Australians were apathetic. She had found them very receptive to migrants who showed that they wanted to become Australians. She had arrived with few educational qualifications and had become the owner of a substantial business. To emphasise her view that Australians are much more flexible and accommodating than others give them credit for, she recalled how she obtained her first job in Sydney. She had seen an advertisement in the local paper for an accounts clerk, went along for an interview and when asked whether she had experience replied that she had worked in an office in Britain. However, as a filing clerk she really did not have the skills necessary to practise as an accounts clerk. Between the time of interview and the date of commencement (only a few days), she went to the local library and consulted all the books she could find on elementary accounting. When she started the job the supervisor recognised both her determination and her lack of experience and for one week sat next to Kathy and taught her all aspects of the job. To Kathy, this was more a sign of improvisation than apathy.

She was particularly critical of the whingeing Pom. When working for a real-estate agency she had met many newly arrived English migrants, some of whom complained bitterly about the country within a few days of arrival. She tried first to appease them, but invariably confronted them and told them that they were being unreasonable and should be ashamed to say that they were British. To one family she said, 'OK, I'll drive you to the airport and put you on the plane if that's what you want. Nobody's keeping you here; just remember you'll have to pay back to the Australian government your fares from Britain. And when you get home you can tell everybody that you stayed in the country for 48 hours and hated it. I'm sure they'll be impressed.'

The determination Kathy had shown before leaving England to settle successfully in Australia was still evident when she was seen 20 years later. She had been back to England only once and was not very happy there. It hadn't changed at all and she realised that she could never live there permanently again. 'I even had nightmares that I got sort of stranded in England and I couldn't get back to Australia', she said. Although she had been teased in a good-natured way by her Australian workmates about her Yorkshire accent, she never showed that their comments hurt, simply because they didn't. By now, probably an acculturated migrant on Richardson's scale, she says that it is the freedom and the opportunity to do what she always wanted to do that has made her identify so strongly with Australia. She believes that had she stayed in England she would never have achieved any of the things she has achieved in Australia, where she has turned her hands to many things and succeeded. Nobody ever asked her about her background. They just presumed that she could do the job. When she decided to establish her present business, she asked her bank manager for a loan and it was given immediately because he was impressed by her achievements, her drive and her determination to succeed. That, she said, would not have been possible in Britain.

*   *   *

'They say life begins at 40; well I'm 39 now, so it will be like a second life. I think it'll be a great experience for both myself and my family.'

117

So said Joe Aspinall, who worked as a bus conductor in Leigh, Lancashire. Together with his wife Mary and five children he had decided to emigrate to Western Australia. Although Joe and Mary had been on the threshold of emigration for almost 17 years, they put the idea aside when they started a family. When the youngest child was five and the others were in school, they decided to emigrate in the hope that they and the children would find a happier and more comfortable livelihood. Mary said that they had 20 or more years to make a good home for themselves and their children in Australia. Neighbours and friends had given them conflicting information about life there, which she had concluded would be like the scenes she had seen in cowboy pictures. She said that if there was dust all over the furniture it couldn't be 'worse than all the sludge that we get here on the kids' shoes and their clothes'.

Joe had been a pitman before becoming a bus conductor. He worked long hours and so had little time to see and get to know his children. He and Mary saved very little from their modest income and considered themselves lucky if they had saved enough to spend an evening in the local club. Since their marriage they had been on holiday only twice.

Boulder lies on Western Australia's fabulous Golden Mile. Since the late nineteenth century, when gold was first discovered in the arid outback of Western Australia, the Golden Mile has yielded hundreds of millions of dollars' worth of gold. Although production has long since passed its peak, the town, established at the turn of the century, did nothing to change Mary's impression that Australian towns were similar to those she had seen in cowboy films. Joe's decision to return to mining (gold not coal) represented an important stage in his new life, for it was destined to be the medium through which he would succeed in achieving the plans he had made to settle his family comfortably in Australia. The voyage out was uneventful, but he spent more money than he should have and so found it difficult to make ends meet during the first few months in Boulder. However, when interviewed after he had been there for five months, Joe said his job paid £30 a week and that his eldest son, who was also working, earned £8 a week. To get that sort of income in the mines in England, said Joe, he would have to do a lot of overtime, including Saturday and Sunday. Now, his weekends and evenings were free; they went to the pictures and the pub frequently. They had even purchased a weatherboard house for £1100;

the bank having required a deposit of only £100 before lending the balance.

Mary reported that the children had quickly adapted to Australian conditions. They were not 'closed in like they had been in England, where if they played football in the street, the neighbours would be annoyed if the ball went into their gardens'. In Australia, said Mary, they could play out in the open spaces without anyone grumbling at them. Joe also thought that the children noticed him more, because he was more accessible than he had been in Leigh.

While Joe and the children were very satisfied with their new life, Mary became extremely homesick and depressed. She said she felt so dead inside; that she was living in a dream. Joe met many people at his work, she said, and the children had many friends at school, but she was left at home on her own. Basically a shy person, she found it difficult to make friends with neighbours. She did not dislike Boulder, but the isolation had made her lonely and homesick. She especially missed her sister's company and her daily visits to her grandmother's place. When she tried to explain to Joe how she felt, he became annoyed. This, she said, was because he was so settled and could see that the children were settled and did not want her homesickness to get so serious that he would have to consider taking her back to England. She therefore realised that she would just have to try to adapt.

When she was reinterviewed in 1987, 20 years after she had first been interviewed in Australia, Mary still recalled vividly the loneliness of those early years in Boulder. In England, she recalled, you knew everyone in the street; there were always people in the gardens to whom you could say 'hello' and have a chat. In addition to the difficulty of making many friends in Boulder, the distances and space were so overwhelming. The streets were enormously long; 'I would go to the gate when the children had gone to school and Joe had gone to work and look up that street and there wasn't a soul in sight that you knew or could talk to. I really got depressed with it all. And then there were those dreadful flies! Our house had only a very small kitchen and it was tin-lined and I cooked on a wood stove'. Cooking meals in midsummer was an ordeal she would never forget. Mary also acknowledged that it was really the future of her five children that kept her in Australia. They adapted to the conditions so easily and quickly. Furthermore, she and Joe did not have the money to repay the outward-passage costs, and the return tickets back. So they just 'knuckled down'.

Joe also remembered his reaction to Mary's inability to settle. It *had* upset him. He used to try to talk things over with her, but this was difficult while she was so depressed. Mary believed that, if she had been a little more pushy, she would have been happier. 20 years later, Mary could say proudly that she really like Australia and being an Australian. She was extremely glad that she had sweated out the difficult early years and had not returned to England. No more does she feel isolated; she has made many friends and is quite content to stay in Australia for the rest of her life.

Joe has adapted to the Australian lifestyle extremely well. He likes Australians because they are good workers and friendly to Englishmen who are prepared to treat them as equals. Since arriving in Australia, the family had achieved much. They had now paid off the mortgage on their home, owned a car and had 'money in the bank'. In England, he said, he could only afford to rent a house, but in Australia, his dream of home-ownership had come true. He was especially glad that the rent collector did not come knocking on his door each week as in England. Following purchase of their first house, they replaced it with another and then another, each being larger because the children needed more space. They then moved from Boulder to a suburb of Perth, where they now live in an attractive three-bedroom bungalow.

Mary and Joe have been back to England on two visits. Although they had lived in a comfortable house in England before emigrating, their reaction to the general environment on return there was that it was so dirty relative to the cleanness and openness of Western Australia's suburbs. And, of course, they missed the sunshine, especially when they got up in the morning to find it was overcast, cold or foggy. They have also travelled to New Zealand on two occasions and to Singapore, and have visited several of their adult children in the eastern states of Australia.

Though happy to remain in Australia for the rest of her life, Mary would not admit to being more Australian than British. She said she was 'half English and half Australian. I would never desert my birthright – I mean I'm still English through and through even though I'm living in Australia'. She still holds a British passport and is not contemplating Australian citizenship.

*   *   *

Having graduated in geology from Hull University, David Hall, with limited prospects for employment in England, accepted a job as a geologist in central Western Australia. His starting salary would be about double what he could earn in Britain. Furthermore, the nominating employer had agreed to provide a house and such facilities as electricity, firewood and a telephone for nominal rent. David already had ambitions for his baby son's future. He did not want him to grow up in cramped living conditions in an environment where families live in terraced houses and children had little space in which to play and develop. In Australia, he would grow up in a big country and know nothing about England. David, however, was not committed to the job he had been offered. He expected it would take three or four years to find out whether or not he liked the country and would make it his home.

Though he did not say so when interviewed in England, David later admitted that he and his wife Josie had heard a lot of stories about how unfriendly Australians were to British migrants. But since being in Australia 'we have not come across any of this'. In fact, Australians had gone out of their way to make them feel welcome. This might have been because he went initially to Gwalia, a hamlet near the small town of Leonora, situated north of Kalgoorlie in central Western Australia. Famous for the Sons of Gwalia goldmine, in which Herbert Hoover, later President of the United States, worked, Gwalia is now home to only a handful of people and has clearly seen better days. Many dwellings are now derelict, shanty houses that once housed hundreds of miners and their families. David's job as geologist often took him away into the country for a week or more. He did not like leaving Josie and their son Carl in a home without telephone and nearby neighbours. But in time he accepted the situation and so did Josie – who, initially, was rather shocked by the environment. Although their house was comfortably furnished, Josie became very lonely and would read and sew a lot to pass the time in David's absence.

David's adaptation to the Australian outback was remarkably rapid. He thought nothing of travelling 150 miles to Kalgoorlie and back to do the weekly shopping. Experience in the outback contributes greatly to character-building, especially traits of toughness and independence. He admitted that the isolated mining camps came as a tremendous shock after the rolling countryside of England. At first the outback's isolation terrified him, especially if he thought about how far he was from another person. If you get lost, you would almost certainly perish, he said.

Josie, a woman of immense character and perseverance, had concluded that migrants should not come to Australia and expect everything to be laid on for them. As a result of his attachment to Australians and their country, David identified himself strongly with Western Australia's mining industry. The circumstances had appealed to David's independent spirit; he liked mine-owners and investors, because, like him, they were prepared to take a calculated gamble.

When reinterviewed in Tasmania 20 years later, Josie was a little more explicit about the difficult conditions she had experienced in Gwalia. During the first week, when their crates and boxes were being unpacked on the verandah of the old home, the temperature reached 115 degrees Fahrenheit every day. There was no air-conditioning, and they would sometimes sit on the verandah with their feet in bowls of cold water. She confirmed that the friendliness and helpfulness of the mining community had done a lot to help her resettle. Josie, like David, is a very independent person. On becoming pregnant during their first few months in Western Australia, she decided that she would have to learn to drive a car so as to get to Leonora, three miles away, should an emergency arise in David's absence. It was also the only way she could make contact with other people and shops. During those early days, several altercations with deadly snakes discovered in and around the house did not endear the Australian countryside to her. Nor did the dust storms that frequently enveloped the whole house.

Like the other families in this quartet, David and Josie returned to England for a visit. This took place in 1969. On their return and disembarkation at Perth airport, they said that they were really thankful to be back in Australia, which they now considered home. Many members of their family have since visited them in Australia, and some have stayed permanently. Josie found herself becoming increasingly homesick with age, especially during the festive season. Both of them are still very close to their family in England; grandparents write frequently and send the children cards and presents. Now successfully integrated migrants, David and Josie have made many friends in the various places that they have settled. Because they have spent all their formative years in Australia, building a career and a family, they identify very strongly with Australia. The only concession that they make to being British is that David would not mind going back to

England to take a job for a short period, provided that it was on a salary comparable to the one he now earns in Tasmania. He is especially impressed by the attitude of Australian mining companies to achievement. Employers prefer geologists who are prepared to get their hands dirty 'and come up with a good idea'. Qualifications, he said, are all very well, but, unless you actually get out and do the job, it doesn't impress Australian employers very much. To them, it's more important to get the job done. As regional exploration manager for his company in Tasmania he carries a great deal of responsibility. Allan Segal, who interviewed David and Josie in Tasmania in 1987, had passed a drilling rig on the journey to David's office. He asked him whether there was any excitement attached to drilling a hole in a specific spot. David's reply tells much about his skills, perseverance and good sense:

Drilling a hole is only the final test; all the years that have gone into the decision: initial conceptual work, ground geology, reconnaissance, gridding, geochemistry, geophysics, sampling, assaying and analysis. You have to put your maps together and, on the basis of all the work you have done, there should be something there, but the only way to find out is to dig a hole.

Chapter 9

Other Migrants Speak: For and Against

The resettlement in Australia of the three families and single woman in the Granada quartet could be considered successful. 22 years after leaving England, they had all declared that Australia would henceforth be their home. Early difficulties of adjustment to the new land, which had been considerable for the wives, had caused much heartache and even led Pat Throssell to persuade her husband Steve to take her home. Others had been back to Britain for holidays but none remained there permanently. For each family, time and their children's ready adaptation to the new country had pushed permanent return from their minds.

Kathy Dolan, and the husbands of the three families, clearly had the personality traits that academics have found to be essential for successful immigrants. Kathy, unencumbered by family responsibilities, applied her great determination to settle successfully in Australia. Joe and Mary Aspinall, older than most migrants when they left England with their five children, had been living in a comfortable home in Leigh, Lancashire. Their initial resettlement was a baptism of fire in more ways than one: life in Western Australia's inland goldfields had been extremely uncomfortable during the summer. Perhaps Mary suffered more from homesickness than any other migrant in the quartet, but Joe's contentment, and the children's rapid adaptation to the new environment, and perhaps the influence of two visits back to England, finally led Mary to declare that she would not settle anywhere else but Australia. Even so, she had not made the final step towards acculturation. She remains a British citizen and describes herself as half Australian and half English.

David Hall, a graduate, was better educated than the others. He emigrated to his first job, also on Western Australia's goldfields. His wife Josie experienced considerable physical hardship in that inhospitable environment, and few Australian women would have been prepared to endure as much. But in those goldfields she also found people with hearts of gold who helped the young mother not only to overcome the physical discomfort of isolation, but also to experience attitudes to life which she readily appreciated and, to a large extent, adopted. David, now a successful mining executive in Tasmania, shared with the other husbands attitudes and a love of country which gained him both the acceptance and the respect of Australians.

Granada had not set out in 1965 to find potentially successful migrants. In many ways it is fortuitous that those chosen succeeded in the way they did; but the Appleyard survey shows that 80 per cent of assisted migrants finally settled in Australia, so the quartet's experiences were not unduly unrepresentative.

In their search for background material prior to leaving Britain in mid 1987 for reinterviews with the Granada migrants, Alison Ray and Allan Segal interviewed many returnees who had resettled in Britain. Some of these persons still considered their Australian experience the worst of their lives; others recalled with fond memories their days in Australia but were also happily settled 'back home'. While in Australia conducting interviews with the Granada quartet, Ray and Segal also saw or tried to arrange to see a number of other former assisted migrants. Some, such as David Hill, the Managing Director of the Australian Broadcasting Corporation, and the entrepreneur, Alan Bond (with whom they were unable to arrange an interview) had become extremely successful. Some had simply come to terms with Australia and stayed there mainly because of their children's proximity and success. Others were as acculturated as Steve and Pat Throssell.

We have already concluded that success as a migrant depends not only upon circumstances encountered in the new country but also on the migrant's own personality and ability to cope with the inevitable difficulties and dislocations posed by resettlement. The permutations of circumstance and personality are limitless. The purpose of this chapter is to provide a pot-pourri of experiences related to Alison Ray and Allan Segal by Britons who had emigrated to Australia under the

126

Assisted Passage Scheme. Some stayed only a short while and returned to Britain, where they have remained every since. Others returned to Britain but regretted their decision not to re-emigrate, and others settled successfully in Australia and returned to Britain only for short visits. Some have achieved much; others (perhaps the majority) have achieved economic circumstances not dissimilar to those they would have experienced had they not left Britain. As will be seen, these people tended to believe that the additional benefits offered by Australia, especially its climate and opportunities for their children, represented the main difference between the two countries, and these benefits were the main reason why they never resettled to Britain.

*   *   *

Keith Judge was a bricklayer who had stood on the threshold of emigration for years. The trigger that pushed him over was the dreadful winter of 1962–3, which lasted from Boxing Day until April. He was a partner in a building company at the time and the bad weather almost sent them bankrupt. A deciding factor in his decision to emigrate was the advice given by a former employee, a house-painter who had worked with Keith on contract jobs. His letters from Australia emphasised how the good weather there never impeded outdoor work. Keith then wrote to Australia House for information, on the basis of which he made his decision to emigrate.

When interviewed back in England in 1987, Keith Judge said it was 'a bloody foolhardy decision to go but I didn't realise it at the time'. During most of his stay in Australia, Keith's income was sufficient only to make ends meet. The hostel to which his family had been allocated in South Australia had no vacancies when they arrived, so they were housed in a temporary building at the back of a hotel. This initial experience made Keith very dissatisfied, and, although his wife seemed less bothered, she was concerned that their child, then only three, could not get rid of a severe cold and might develop pneumonia. More important, the Judges felt let down by the firm that had nominated them. The promise of flat-type accommodation did not materialise. Soon after they arrived, their friend visited them and, appalled by the standard of their accommodation, arranged for them to rent a farm-house. Although they enjoyed the outdoor life, Keith remained very concerned that his nominator (a building company) still had not offered him employment. Apparently the job offer was conditional upon his purchasing one of the company's properties. He severed his connection with the company and searched for employment through newspaper advertisements. He was appalled by advertisements containing such sentences as 'Poms need not apply'.

Despite the offer of a job for his wife from a friend who owned a delicatessen, Keith had by then decided that he had had enough. He was not earning as much as he had been earning in England and believed that he had been misled by the wages quoted in response to his enquiries at Australia House. It was not so much the information concerning wages that was misleading as the fact that prices quoted for laying bricks assumed that the bricklayer would provide his own barrow, scaffolding, and so on. The difficulties Keith had encountered trying to find a job, and his forthright reaction to what he believed was misleading information given by Australia House, caused him to criticise most things Australian. Perhaps his own attitude contributed to what he said was a great deal of anti-British prejudice in Australia. He resented Australians who responded to criticism with the standard advice, 'If England is so bloody marvellous what are you doing here?' Experiences of shady deals with furniture and car-dealers only exacerbated the Judges' disappointments. They were not bothered by ants, spiders and flies, but they were bothered by the attitudes of Australians.

The Judges returned to England in November 1963, having emigrated in June the same year. Keith recalled with some bitterness that he had to repay to the Australian government the cost of their outward passages. He said that he had gone to Australia with £1700 and returned with £175. On return he had no house, no job, no bed to sleep on and three children at school. His one word of implied goodwill towards Australia was that on return to England he was more motivated to succeed and create a good business than he had been before he left. If I hadn't gone to Australia, he said, I probably would have sat around regretting the decision for many years thereafter.

*   *   *

Bill Scurrah was demobilised from the Royal Air Force at the age of 22, and obtained a job as a miner in the north of England but found it difficult to settle into civvy life. He made enquiries about emigrating to

Canada, New Zealand and Australia, but finally decided on Australia because of the Assisted Passage Scheme. The voyage out on an old steamer was not pleasant and the £5 that Bill had in his pocket when he left had diminshed to twopence when he reached Melbourne docks. With no contact in Australia and nowhere to go, he approached a policeman and asked for suggestions. The policeman realised that Bill had lived in a town close to the town he had come from in Cumbria, and so gave him advice which led to his getting a job at Broken Hill, a mining town in western New South Wales.

Bill's first contact with Australians was memorable: a punch-up when a workmate called him a Pommy bastard. Bill was also appalled at the so-called 'six o'clock swill'. In those days, Australian hotels closed at 6 p.m. and some workers were in the habit of leaving work at 4.30 and drinking as much as they could until the pub closed. He met and married his wife Eve in Australia. In 1958 they returned to Cumbria for a three-month honeymoon. His wife fell in love with Bill's village and seemingly its people with her. So they stayed there for four years before returning to Broken Hill in 1962 to visit Eve's family. Within a few months Eve, the Australian, was homesick for Cumbria. Despite her constant requests to Bill to take her back to England, they stayed a further ten years, during which they had two more Australian children. When Bill's mother became seriously ill, they returned to Cumbria, where they stayed for nearly ten years. In 1982, when the children had left school, they decided to return to Australia yet again, where they established a hotel near the South Australian–New South Wales border. Because of different licensing and gambling laws in South Australia and New South Wales, 80 per cent of the hotel's trade comprised travellers from South Australia who came to Broken Hill to gamble on poker machines. However, when the gambling laws were changed, the hotel business declined dramatically. In January 1987, they decided to sell and return to England. Eve had always wanted to retire in the village, and now that the children were grown up they were finally able to do what they had always wanted to do. She loves the village and, while she may return to Australia again, it will only be to see her children.

Looking back over their long and unusual migration experience, Bill thought that Australians are now a lot more tolerant of British migrants than during the 1950's. It took many years for even his in-laws to accept him, because of the stigma that the whingeing Pom had created in

129

Australia. 'They were in the minority' said Bill, 'but shit sticks.' He firmly believed that the time it took to be accepted by Australians was due largely to the negative opinions created by whingeing Poms. When acceptance finally arrived it was worth waiting for. He admits that during his first two years in Australia he hated everything and everyone. It was not until he realised that he was the one out of step that he began to come to terms with the requirements of successful settlement in Australia.

★   ★   ★

Ian and Molly Earwaker left their home in Bath largely because Ian's wage as a plasterer was simply insufficient to make ends meet. Molly was the initiator of the venture and it was undertaken on the understanding that if Ian did not like Australia they would return. As they had owned their house in Bath, they were able to take over £1000 capital to Australia. The Earwakers had been sponsored by a housing company in Australia on the understanding that they would buy one of the company's new houses at Elizabeth, South Australia. After one or two difficulties with employment, Ian finally found a good job which paid £27 a week, compared to the £7–9 he was earning in England. He went into partnership with another plasterer and at one stage was earning $A1000 a week. The couple saved enough money to purchase a 300-acre farm in South Australia seven years after they had arrived.

The Earwakers were victims of the disastrous bushfires in South Australia in 1983. They lost everything – cowsheds, haysheds, cattle and most of the house. This terrifying experience led them to vow never to live on an Australian farm again. Ian remembered every detail of the fateful day: 'We saw the fire coming towards us and we filled up buckets of water in the bath which we threw all over the house to try and stop it burning. Then it started to get really smoky; we actually sat in the house surrounded by water as the fire went through and destroyed it. We only survived by climbing into the bath full of water. I honestly thought that it was the end.' They spent two days in hospital recovering from burnt eyes and parched throats. The blistered skin on Ian's face peeled for days thereafter. While the Earwakers may go back to Australia, they would not settle on the farm, which is now rented. They have concluded that Australia is a country for anyone who is prepared to work. It gave them a great start, they enjoyed the weather and were at ease with Australians, who, said Molly, are a lot more down-to- earth than most other people.

*   *   *

Dreenagh Durrell, who now lives in England, has no intention of ever going back to Australia. She had emigrated with her parents and six siblings from Belfast when she was 11 years of age. Her father had been completely taken by the propaganda and was convinced that the streets of Australia were paved with gold. As he was an impossibly adventurous man, the prospect of emigrating to Australia for a mere £20 was too great a temptation to resist. 'My father made up his mind very quickly', said Dreenagh, 'and – all of a sudden – we were off.' The venture began poorly. Their ship, the P & O *Strathmore*, was on its last voyage. They were travelling steerage and below the water line. The ship had no stabilisers and in the Bay of Biscay they were all as sick as dogs. On arrival in Melbourne, they were transferred on to what she described as a very ancient train for the overnight journey to Smithville Hostel in Adelaide. Conditions there, she said, were 'absolutely horrendous'. The food served in a communal dining hall was of very poor quality. Because her mother complained so bitterly, the family was moved to another hostel in Adelaide.

Dreenagh developed very negative attitudes about Australia and Australians. She found a great deal of anti-British prejudice. She disagreed that the term 'Pommy bastard' had any element of endearment, but acknowledged that it was often used against those who complained unnecessarily. Her father never liked Australia and so the family decided to move to New Zealand, which she described as even worse than Australia. Dreenagh returned to Sydney, stayed a while, and returned to Britain with her Australian boyfriend. After some time there, she was persuaded by her boyfriend to return to Australia, which she says was the one big mistake of her life. She lived in Melbourne, then Sydney, where she went to university and on graduation obtained a job in television from which she saved money to 'get the hell out of Australia never to return'. Dreenagh's negative attitudes to Australia were conveyed by her final comment: 'The thing that really got me at the end was the whole hype about Australia: how wonderful Australia is – and it's not. The only passion in Australia is for beer, football and barbecues, but that's all. There is no conversation except about football, beer and betting and there's no general conversation when you meet people over dinner.'

*   *   *

The thing that decided Barry Fewters and his wife to leave Australia was the attitude of its people. Like most people going to Australia, he said they had been sold on the idea of leisure, beaches and sun. Indeed, the picture painted for him by Australia House was that he was going to a land of opportunity where there wasn't anything you couldn't do if you were prepared to put your mind to it and work hard. He had been swept along by the groundswell of opinion in favour of Australia during the mid-1960s. Though he was not dissatisfied with life in England, he wanted something better and thought that Australia could provide it. Having recently been married, he thought that his wife and baby daughter would find better opportunities there. The £10 passage made it so easy to fulfil his adventurous ambitions.

The Fewters flew to Australia and were taken directly to Wacol Hostel in Brisbane. Their first reaction was 'absolutely awful': the Nissen huts had been partitioned and the walls were so flimsy that you could hear what your neighbours were thinking. Communal washing facilities and the hostel environment were very distressing. Barry's wife spent the first two days crying and demanding to return home. They moved out of the hostel within a few weeks and rented a house in Brisbane. What upset them most during those early days was the insects. Most migrants had been attracted to Australia by propaganda about the coast, surfing, swimming, the bronzed people and the sunshine. But they were not told about the 'horrendous number of insects, ants and flies'. The old wooden house they shared with another English family had been built on stilts and was 'alive with bugs and cockroaches'. Barry recalled the occasion when his wife noticed an enormous dead cockroach on the bathroom floor being carried off by the ants. She also complained that you couldn't possible open the windows of the house at night, because if you did all the bugs and moths would fly in, attracted by the light. 'People think this is bullshit, but you could actually hear the moths thumping against the windows at night.'

Nor were his experiences in employment satisfactory; he changed jobs frequently and often because of difficulties with workmates and employers. Barry said he experienced constant anti-British feeling in Australia. He was regularly called a Pommy bastard, not so much by Australians who had visited England but by younger Australians who thought that all Englishmen walked around in pin-striped suits and sat on the beach with their trousers rolled up and knotted handkerchiefs on their heads. He admitted that basically he did not get on with Australians. He felt he was constantly having to defend England from attack by Australians, who knew nothing about the country but pretended that they did. The typical Australian attitude was that Britons only came out to Australia to get a good feed and that they kept coal in the bath. You can only stand that for so long, he said, and then you find yourself fighting back and defending things which you know are your own and it turned me into a patriot. I knew what it was like to live in London, but they've never been there and I was not about to allow them to rubbish it.

The most pleasant experience Barry recalled about living in Maribyrnong Hostel, which was like living in a garden shed, was the companionship he shared with other English people in the hostel. Other English migrants were the only people he made friends with. He recalled how they would sit around in one of the rooms talking about England – English streets, English pubs and anything that had appeared on the news that day relating to England. It took their minds off the dreadful hostel and all the things he didn't like about Australia. When they finally decided to return to England, other English people from the hostel came to see them off. His wife was so pleased to be leaving Australia, he said, that as she was waving goodbye to friends on the dockside she literally fainted and fell back in his arms. She fainted, he said, with the sheer pleasure of going back to England.

*   *   *

Michael Beaumont emigrated to Australia in 1967. He had left school when he was 17 years old to work as a clerk in an insurance office. After about 18 months he got what he described as the Wanderlust, applied to emigrate to Australia and was accepted. The advertisements he saw made the country look so romantic, vast and full of adventure. Being under 21, he needed his parents' permission. His mother was not too happy to give it, but his father, although reluctant, did not stand in his way. He was sponsored to Australia by the Big Brother Movement and carried a letter of introduction to his former employer's Australian office. He disliked the communal living required under the Big Brother scheme and soon left their hostel in Sydney to share a flat at Kensington, one of Sydney's eastern suburbs, with friends. He obtained a job with his former employer's Sydney office and within six weeks had moved to a flat near the beach. Michael described this period of his life as pure magic. Though he loved Australia, in the back of his mind was the possibility, told him by Australia House before leaving, that he would be eligible for military service. Under the Australian National Service system that existed at the time, all young men had to register for service during the six months preceding their twentieth birthday. A ballot was held to decide who would be called for national service. Michael, to his consternation, was selected. He was sent to Wagga Wagga, a town in New South Wales, for basic training, which he found rather difficult because as a youth he had never been subject to any real discipline. After ten weeks of basic training he was sent to a battalion base camp in Townsville, where the jungle training routine was one of the hardest in the world. In May 1969 Michael was shipped to Vietnam with the advance party of the Sixth Battalion. He was stationed at Nuidat, the base for Australian troops. His platoon would go out on patrol for a month at a time. They were taken to the Mekong delta, where they spent four weeks on patrol. On return to camp they were given 36 hours leave and returned to camp for seven or eight days before going out on another mission. The whole experience was something Michael did not want to talk about, although he did admit that it was kinder to him than to a lot of other people. There were a lot of casualties and he always seemed to be in the wrong place at the wrong time.

On his return to Australia he decided to fly to Canada with a friend and then to England where his parents were greatly relieved to see him. Michael recalls being on a 'high' for a long time after coming out of Vietnam. He described the experience as being the ultimate drug and estimates that it took him more than two years to get over the experience. 'There's not a week goes by that I don't have some recollection of it. It's too vivid to forget.' Michael stayed in Britain for 18 months and returned to Australia in January 1972. He returned to his job with the insurance company but found it difficult to settle down after the Vietnam experience. On the premature death of his father in

England, he returned and lived with his mother. On finding a good job as a sales representative, he decided to stay in England.

★   ★   ★

Although the number of returnees, re-emigrants and re-returnees is considerable, the characteristic assisted British migrant is the one who remains in Australia and makes several visits back to England on holidays. The following experiences relate to four such persons.

★   ★   ★

Peter Smith arrived in Sydney in 1961 with his parents, two sisters and a brother. The family had lived in West Hartlepool in the north-east of England. He now lives in Adelaide and is a major in the Australian Army. Though only four when he left England, he remembers many tears being shed by his parents as they left their terraced home for Australia. Peter's father had been a soldier and was used to communal living, although his mother could never get used to lining up for food at the hostel where they lived in Sydney. She burst into tears when they arrived at the hostel and asked to be taken back to England. She enjoyed neither the hostel communal life nor the insects and animals surrounding the hostel. Seeing lizards scampering over the rocks made her think she had been taken back to prehistoric days. The family moved several times before settling in a Housing Commission house in Liverpool, New South Wales. Peter won a bursary to go to a private school and on graduation obtained a job as a reporter on an Australian newspaper before joining the Army.

When Peter returned to West Hartlepool in 1984 with his wife, he couldn't believe the conditions under which his grandmother was living in the old terraced house. He felt so guilty that he gave her financial assistance. 'We had spent thousands of dollars on the trip and could virtually afford anything we wanted and here was my grandmother living in a hole.' Peter now considers himself an Australian. 'I owe this country too much to call myself an Englishman. I'm totally assimilated. I love the country. I think it is the best country on earth – we don't know how lucky we are.' He is always embarrassed by whingeing Poms, whom he tells to go back to their council houses and snow. There is no way that Peter would consider returning to England. He believes that he has become totally assimilated.

*　　　*　　　*

Though David Hill, Managing Director of the Australia Broadcasting Corporation, is one of Australia's leading opinion-makers, he began life in a 'three-up and three-down roomed house in Eastbourne'. He has a twin and an elder brother. His mother, whom he describes as a totally unskilled woman, tried to raise four children in the austere conditions of post-war Britain. Overwhelmed by the task, her children were placed into homes on the understanding that she would reclaim them when she recovered. From Dr Barnardo's home in Barkingside, Essex, they were sent to Australia under Fairbridge Society sponsorship. Thus, at the tender age of 12, David left England on the P & O liner *Strathaird*. The voyage was something David could never have visualised in his wildest dreams:

> We arrived at Tilbury at four o'clock in the afternoon and it was a cold March, so-called spring day. They said we had to hurry up because it was tea time. We thought, cor, it's early for having tea, on the grounds that you had breakfast, dinner and tea and nothing more until the following morning. All they served was bread and jam and marmite. We went back to our cabins knowing that this was 'it'. But then the bell started ringing for dinner. We were totally confused. Dinner? We had tea, how could we have dinner? So went downstairs and had dinner – an eight-course meal. We, and most of the migrants on the ship, were still getting the old Raj service. At 7.30 in the morning there was a gentle knock on the door and the steward came in with a cup of tea and a biscuit and if you took sugar he stirred it for you.

David Hill said that they were lucky because they had been placed in a state cabin in what had been the first-class section of the ship. They were also on the 'posh' side (port-side outward, starboard home). It was a voyage in unbelievable luxury. He and his brother sat like two little Lord Fauntleroys in enormous armchairs in the first-class lounge. They had never been served drinks with ice before. 'Everything was so big, of course, because I was only twelve.' *Strathaird* arrived at Sydney harbour on a cold and rainy day. With his two brothers, Richard and Dudley, the Hill boys proceeded to accommodation provided by Fairbridge at Molong in New South Wales. After meeting the principal they were taken down to the cottage which would be their home. David Hill recalls with absolute clarity the squalor of the place. The cottage mother was away at the time and the 15 boys who lived there had created an awful mess; smelly clothing was lying all over the place. At 5 a.m. they were woken by a bare light bulb. Around them were bare floorboards, no cupboards, just shelves for clothes.

Discipline at the farm was very strict. Conditions were very primitive and the leaders very insensitive. Before leaving for school, the boys had to do chores around the farm. The whole ethos was, he said, anti-education: boys were being trained to become farmhands and girls were being trained to become farmers' wives. Fairbridge Farm, he said, had simply outlived its time. Some of the senior children went to school in Molong, but the others stayed on the farm until they were 17. On leaving the farm they had no experience of life outside. David Hill left for Sydney when he was 15 and obtained a job immediately. He recalls going to the employment office in North Sydney and being asked how much education he'd had. He replied 'none' and so the official drew cards from the drawer of a filing cabinet labelled 'Jobs for unskilled, unemployed boys aged fifteen'. He was asked which job he wanted. When David asked for the one that was nearest he was told to report to an office around the corner. So began his working life as a shop assistant in a hardware store in Crows Nest. Clearly a man of burning ambition, he matriculated for entry to university, studied during the day and worked as a waiter and pub bouncer at night. Although he recalls the early difficult years at Fairbridge with some anguish, David Hill is now firmly settled in Australia. He believes that he could never have achieved in Britain what he has achieved in Australia. Australia, he says, does not have the resistance to social mobility and the appalling inequality that exists in Britain. One of the most important things about Australian society, he said, is that somebody from his environment, coming to Australia through the Fairbridge scheme, could, and did, become the head first of the New South Wales railway system and then of the Australian Broadcasting Corporation.

★   ★   ★

Philip Hockney had been working in Bradford, Yorkshire, for a company that built petrol tankers. Though dissatisfied with his job, he found it difficult to obtain another in that part of England. The only jobs he could fill were in the south and he realised that if he sold his house and moved there the cost of replacing it would be much greater than the return obtained from the sale of his Bradford house. The idea of moving to Australia for a couple of years, without commitment to permanent settlement, attracted both Philip and his wife Mary. They hoped to make some money and, possibly, return to England and obtain employment in the south.

He recalls that the information provided by Australia House was not very helpful because it did not address his specific skills and requirements. The adventure did not get off to a good start. They sailed to Australia on an Italian ship. Mary was allocated a four-berth cabin with their baby daughter and three other women and Philip was allocated a cabin with other men. The food was not appetising and they resented having to share bathroom facilities.

They were met by friends in Sydney and taken on a tour of the city before arriving at Cabramatta Migrant Hostel. Their new home was a Nissen hut. The walls, made of plywood, stopped 18 inches from the ceiling and so, recalls Philip they knew when the couple on the other side of the partition were making love. It was pathetic. The first morning he made enquiries at the employment office at the hostel and was sent from one office to another because the clerks were not used to placing in employment persons with professional skills. Philip then made his own contacts by phoning companies that manufactured tanks. He was placed in touch with an employer who needed a draughtsman with Philip's skills but not at that time, so he offered him £25 a week doing other work. His all-round skills and training as a draughtsman stood him in good stead in Australia, because his employer expected him to do a number of activities relating to draughtsmanship. Following a number of mishaps relating to housing, Philip and Mary finally returned to a migrant hostel for another three years before succeeding in acquiring a house of their own. Finally, a company representative who visited them in the hostel was so appalled by the conditions that he arranged for the company to provide a guaranteed loan so that the Hockneys could shift to a house.

In 1967 Phil established his own business with two partners. After a number of difficulties relating to a contract with his former employer, he bought out his partners and began his own engineering firm, which later became Hockney Alcan. To get established, he borrowed money from a number of banks. The company prospered and by 1974 he was employing about 150 people, had an assembly plant in Brisbane and a factory in Sydney. In 1983 his former employer bought 40 per cent of his company. He is now able to assemble trucks for his former employer as well as build tankers for other companies.

The Australian situation allowed Phil to make progress which he thinks would have been difficult to match in Britain. Now a very successful entrepreneur, this migrant thinks he may have been a little ahead of his time. Though his financial fingers have occasionally been burnt, he says that overall everything has worked out well. He is quite relaxed about being called a Pom and usually gives as much banter as he gets. He is firmly of the view that Australia is a classless society, perhaps the most classless society in the world. He has never experienced prejudice of any kind in business dealings. He and Mary have become naturalised Australians and have no intention of ever returning to England. They call themselves an Australian family, with three Australian grandchildren. Their two married daughters are as happily settled as Philip and Mary.

Chapter 10
Balance Sheet and Conclusion

Although Australia's immigration policy has progressively stripped British immigrants of the many privileges they once enjoyed relative to other nationalities, the British base is firmly entrenched in Australia's demographic structure. Even if the diverse ethnic mix of contemporary immigration to Australia continues for another 25 years, the British element will still be approximately 70 per cent of the population.

Assessing the overall economic, demographic and social contribution made by post-war British migrants to Australia is a daunting task. Aside from having to unravel from annual statistics the number of second- and third-time re-emigrants, as well as the *bona fide* Australians who were born in Britain while their parents were visiting the country, it is almost impossible to identify assisted from non-assisted British migrants once they have settled in Australia.

Adult assisted migrants generally did not change their occupations after arrival, but many of their British-born dependent children entered the Australian education system and later obtained appropriate technical or tertiary skills. To this British contribution to Australian society must also be added the achievements of the migrants' Australian-born children. In this regard, the Australian census of 1986, which sought for the first time information on the numbers and characteristics of Australians according to the birthplace of their parents, indicated that, in addition to the 1,127,196 persons born in the United Kingdom and Ireland, there were 329,994 Australian-born persons whose parents had been born in those countries. A further 931,412 Australian-born persons had one parent who had been born in those countries. In other words, of the 15.6 million Australians in 1986,

141

2.4 million (or 15 per cent) had either been born in the United Kingdom and Ireland or had one or both parents who had been born there.

Earlier censuses conducted in Australia confirm the impressive contributions made by British migrants to Australia's economic and demographic development. While it is not possible to separate assisted from non-assisted migrants, and the statistics of persons born in the United Kingdom include migrants who arrived in Australia before the Second World War, the mere fact that probably 80 per cent of post-war British migrants to Australia have been assisted suggest that data on British-born persons in Australia will be dominated by former assisted migrants. As already noted, non-assisted British migrants have characteristically been persons of high socio-economic class whose employers in Australia have paid their outward fares. They are therefore more likely to be represented in the professional and business categories than are assisted migrants. In 1981, when the Assisted Passage Scheme had been all but dismantled, there were 1.08 million persons born in the United Kingdom and Ireland residing in Australia. This represents slightly less than 10 per cent of the total population. About 890,000 of these persons had been born in England, of whom 51 per cent were aged 15–44. Those who had arrived between 1975 and 1981 had not been disproportionately drawn from any particular region of the United Kingdom. This confirms the situation described by Appleyard in relation to assisted British migrants in 1958–9. Although most of the British-born migrants still live in the two most populous states (New South Wales and Victoria), higher proportions, relative to the state's total population reside in Western Australia and South Australia. For example, in the outer suburbs of Perth the percentage of British- and Irish-born persons exceeded 20 per cent of the district's population: Kwinana, 36 per cent; Rockingham, 33 per cent; Armadale, 37 per cent; and Gosnells, 24 per cent. In Elizabeth, South Australia, which on its establishment during the 1950s attracted many British migrant families, 33 per cent of the 1981 population had been born in the United Kingdom and Ireland. The family emphasis of the Assisted Passage Scheme is clearly conveyed by statistics on sex ratios. In 1981 there were 103 English-born males for every 100 English-born females. Between 1947 and 1960, about 115,000 grooms who had been born in England and Wales married Australian-born brides, and over 80,000 brides born in England and Wales married Australian-born grooms.

Clearly, there has been a great deal of intermarriage between the two nationalities.

The economic contribution made by British migrants has been especially impressive. The 1981 census showed that 10 per cent of males aged 15 or over who had been born in the British Isles held higher degrees or diplomas, compared with only 8.6 per cent of Australian-born males. The respective percentages for those holding trade certificates were 21 and 17 per cent, a statistic that Lucas suggests reflects selective recruiting by Australian employers as well as immigration requirements. 14 per cent of males born in England and Wales and aged 15 or over had professional and technical occupations at the 1981 census, compared with 11.9 per cent of Australian-born males. Also, 41 per cent were classified in 'trades', compared with 37 per cent for Australian-born males.

After 1970, the proportion of professional and skilled persons in the immigration intake from the United Kingdom increased substantially. Between 1967 and 1973, 22 per cent of male settlers from the United Kingdom and Ireland had such skills, compared with 38 per cent for the period 1976–8. Unemployment rates for British migrants have also generally been lower than rates for migrants from other countries. This reflects not only their skill mix but also the criteria set down in the Assisted Passage Scheme and the general acceptance by Australian employers of British professional and trade qualifications. Female workers born in the United Kingdom and Ireland had workforce participation rates similar to Australian-born females.

Impressive though the formal contributions of British migrants to Australia have been, this book has been concerned primarily with the background, achievements and resettlement of persons who entered Australia between 1947 and 1982 under the United Kingdom–Australia Assisted Passage Agreements. Assisted migration from Britain to Australia was strongly supported by Australian governments for many decades. The British government became financially involved in such schemes only after the First World War, when it saw great advantages in establishing a common market among the Dominions. This led to the implementation of preferential trade agreements and capital-grant arrangements between the United Kingdom and the Dominions, as well as financial support for assisted migration.

Although the inter-war assisted-migration scheme was not entirely successful, Australia reactivated the scheme after the Second World

War, when it launched an immigration programme designed to enhance the nation's defence and economic development. The numbers of immigrants entering Australia each year thereafter would be equal to 1 per cent of the Australian population. The first Minister for Immigration, Arthur Calwell, launched the programme on the basis that British immigrants would be accorded the highest priority. His personal hope was that there would be 10 British migrants for every 'foreigner'. However, Calwell's hope never came close to being realised. While interest by Britons in emigrating to Australia (especially under the Assisted Passage Scheme implemented in 1947) was enormous, and applications far exceeded the number of immigrants required by Australia under its '1 per cent of population' policy, this interest was not converted into emigrants.

First, shipping shortages, due to enormous losses during the war, prevented all but a few thousand Britons from going to Australia during the early post-war years. Calwell worked feverishly to try and resolve the problem, proposing an array of schemes, many of which were successful. Collectively, his negotiations with the British government and British shipping companies secured 25,000 berths for assisted migrants in 1948. Thereafter, an array of special arrangements, including the acquisition of a large passenger liner (with British government support) and long-term agreements with non-British shipping companies to provide migrants-only vessels, reduced the constraints shipping placed on the success of the scheme.

Second, because Calwell soon saw that these problems would greatly restrict the numbers of British assisted emigrants coming to Australia, he pursued a contingency plan under which non-British Europeans would supplement the British intake to required levels. The availability of displaced persons in European refugee camps for resettlement overseas led Calwell to sign an agreement with the International Refugee Organisation. Between 1948 and 1952 over 170,000 displaced persons entered Australia under that programme. They were transported on ships provided by the International Refugee Organisation and under conditions which Calwell considered were unsuitable for 'our kith and kin'. However, planning of this kind was not simply a numbers game. British skilled workers, readily employable in Australia, filled jobs necessary for Australia's post-war economic development; displaced persons were directed to fill unskilled jobs. This

144

'balance' went a long way towards meeting Australia's early post-war labour requirements.

The enormous interest shown by Britons in emigrating to Australia during the first post-war decade reflected to some extent shortages and rationing at home relative to the abundance and opportunities offered by Australia. A very large number of Britons, sympathetic to the patriotism and generosity of Australians in their time of need, saw the country as a sunny, prosperous land where a man could earn much higher wages and not be bound in his spending by a network of officially devised restrictions. The typical Briton probably also thought that Australia was a classless society where achievement was not dependent upon breeding, background or education. It was also a 'British' country where English was spoken, a friendly place where Britons would be welcomed as brothers.

The Assisted Passage Scheme, originally funded equally by the Australian and British governments, gave Britons the opportunity to find a niche in this Shangri-La. But, aside from the dearth of ships necessary to transport selected migrants to Australia, only a small proportion of the estimated 400,000 Britons who had registered at Australia House for assisted passages by November 1947 could be selected. The Australian government, though tempted to take the 'cream' of applicants, honoured its obligation under the agreement to take a 'cross-section' of the British population. Initially, the civilian scheme gave priority to personally nominated migrants whose nominators were required to provide accommodation. During the 1950s, the Commonwealth Nomination Scheme was implemented, under which skilled persons were nominated by the Australian Government and placed in hostel-type accommodation in Australia.

While the Australian government's enthusiasm for the Assisted Passage Scheme never wavered, the same could not be said for the British government. Adverse demographic trends, losses of able-bodied workers during the war, and the high demand for labour to reconstruct war-damaged property and provide dollar-earning exports combined to dampen its enthusiasm for the scheme. As early as 1946, there were signs that the British government was relatively disinterested in participating as an equal financial partner in the scheme. Though statements of general support were made by Prime Minister Attlee and his ministers, it was Winston Churchill's outburst in 1947, implying that Britons who emigrated could be likened to rats leaving a

145

sinking ship, that set a mood which thereafter permeated British support for the scheme.

The British government's response to the Assisted Passage Scheme contrasted with the enormous enthusiasm shown by Australian governments and institutions. Citizenship Conventions held in Canberra during the 1950s were occasions for ministers to lead an orchestra of dedicated and unwavering musicians drawn from all sectors of Australian society. Churches, trade unions, businessmen and sports organisations gave strong support to the immigration programme in general and British immigration in particular. By then, the British proportion of immigration had settled at around 50 per cent, the remainder coming from other European countries. Because few delegates at the Conventions believed that British immigrants (most of whom had been sponsored by their relatives) found it very difficult to resettle in Australia, the Conventions were mainly concerned with resettlement problems experienced by 'foreigners'.

In many ways, both direct and indirect, British migrants were persistently accorded much better deals (assisted passages, good job opportunities and general acceptance by the Australians) than were other migrants. There was a thread of condescension in the comments made by ministers and others on the important roles being played in nation-building by 'New Australians'. British migrants, on the other hand, were the centrepiece of the programme – kith and kin who were helping to preserve Australia's links with the motherland. One event that sparked a re-examination of the British contribution to Australia's development was the government's decision to begin the Commonwealth Nomination Scheme, under which the nominees were accommodated initially in migrant hostels. These were usually former army camps or unused warehouses that had been converted into accommodation modules, and where migrants had communal meals and shared all facilities. They were designed principally as transition dwellings. However, extremely high demand for housing in Australia at the time reduced the supply of private dwellings for rent and forced banks to insist that potential borrowers for housing provide substantial deposits. Many Commonwealth-nominated British migrants, especially those who had large families and had arrived in Australia with only a few hundred pounds, were unable to compete effectively with Australians for the few rented houses or to save the required deposit.

The migrant hostels became places of great unhappiness and unrest.

Wives in particular felt locked into situations from which there was little chance of escape. They met few Australians; their day-to-day contact was with migrant wives in similar circumstances, which only exacerbated their disappointment and distress. At the 1957 Citizenship Convention, Gough Whitlam, the Opposition spokesman on immigration, disturbed what had been a cosy back-slapping event for nearly a decade with his attack not only on the declining British proportion of the immigration intake, but also on the Liberal government's employment, housing and social-security policies, which had caused British migrants so much difficulty during their early days in Australia. Commonwealth hostels became the prime target of attack; everyone, it seemed, agreed that something should be done to alleviate the problems being experienced by British migrants in those hostels, where some had stayed for several years. The next Convention (1958) was important for another reason. W.D. Borrie, the eminent Australian demographer, warned delegates not only that Britain was not an inexhaustible reservoir of potential migrants, but also that, because of the high degree of cultural and institutional similarity between Britain and Australia, immigration flows would always be in a situation of 'extremely delicate poise'. This, he said, had contributed to a significant circular flow of migrants (i.e. return migration) between the two countries. By 1958 Britons could obtain assisted passages with greater ease than in early post-war years. Many more persons were therefore coming to Australia on assisted passages without commitment to stay as permanent settlers, and this produced increased rates of return. Some migrants, as the evidence in this book has shown, travelled back and forth between the two countries, unable to decide in which to settle.

Throughout the 1950s, Australian governments had clearly been more enthusiastic about participating in the Assisted Passage Scheme than British governments, even though opinion polls conducted in Britain during the period showed that an incredible number of persons would emigrate to another country 'if free to do so'. The proportion ranged from 28 and 40 per cent of the persons polled, increasing if the polls were taken during periods of political or economic crisis such as the Berlin airlift, the Korean War and the Suez crisis. In such periods, many Britons who had been on the threshold of emigration for some time, unable to make up their minds, decided to emigrate.

Even though well over a million Britons emigrated to Australia under the Assisted Passage Scheme, little is known about their backgrounds, reasons for emigrating and how they fared in Australia. The Appleyard survey, conducted with over 800 families and single assisted emigrants between 1959 and 1967, provided some answers. Though the replies given by the sampled emigrants relate only to the 1959 'cohort', the survey revealed *processes* of decision-making and resettlement that were probably typical of the experience of assisted emigrants throughout the life of the scheme. Assisted emigrants were by no means the outcasts of British society. The selection procedures alone assured that they met basic criteria relating to skills, age, family composition and so on. The families in the study were, in many respects, average working-class British families who lived in semi-detached or terraced houses. The husbands earned on average £13 sterling a week for 49 hours' work. Predominantly Anglican or nonconformist in religion, they expected to transfer, after sale of assets, an average £289 to Australia.

The survey confirmed earlier research which had suggested that emigrants had different traits and attitudes from non-emigrants. They were more willing to better themselves, less prepared to accept their 'lot' without question, more enterprising and less attached to Britain. They had characteristically stood on the threshold of emigration for many years before some trigger (such as redundancy or a personal disappointment, combined often with the willingness of a relative in Australia to sponsor them) decided them to step across. The majority had become potential emigrants because they believed Australia offered a higher standard of living and better opportunities for advancement than Britain. Other reasons, such as Australia's better climate, tended to be secondary in importance. Many also believed that Britain's class system and social structure would prevent their children from fulfilling their potential if they stayed. Yet, despite these lofty and often rationalised responses, probably only a fraction of these Britons would have emigrated to Australia had it not been for the availability of near-free transport under the Assisted Passage Scheme. Indeed, given their average capital transfer, most emigrants would have had to borrow money in order to pay their and their families' fares to Australia.

One of the prime goals that emigrants hoped to attain in Australia was home ownership. To many it represented an achievement and independence that seemed an impossible dream in Britain. Their

148

knowledge of Australia was surprisingly accurate concerning such important aspects of settlement as wage rates, housing costs and social security. Large families sponsored under the Commonwealth Nomination Scheme scored especially well in this regard.

Follow-up interviews with the migrants when they had been in Australia for about 21 months, and again when they had been there for six years (or, if they had returned to Britain, after the same lapse of time), provided insights into their processes of assimilation. Initial resettlement varied considerably according to whether they had been nominated by a relative, and therefore were initially accommodated in his home, or whether they had been nominated by the Commonwealth government and therefore placed in a hostel. In assessing the migrants' adaptation to Australia over the six-year period, I had the advice and support of Nightingale the economist and Richardson the social psychologist. The latter included on the interview schedules several key questions that made it possible to locate the migrant on a scale of assimilation from satisfaction to identification and acculturation (SIA).

Nightingale was able to show quite conclusively that in their first jobs in Australia migrants enjoyed a significant increase in real income over what they had earned in their last jobs in Britain. However, the cost of replacing, or buying for the first time, consumer durables, and especially the cost of a deposit on a house and mortgage repayments, left them with little cash for the purchase of non-perishable goods. To ease their early financial difficulties, many wives who had not intended working before they emigrated entered the workforce, provided they could make satisfactory arrangements for the care of their children. By 1967, however, migrants still in Australia had generally achieved the economic objectives they had set themselves before departure. Nearly 60 per cent owned or were buying their houses, generally detached bungalows containing three bedrooms; their incomes had also kept pace with Australian wage rates.

Estimating non-economic aspects of their resettlement predictably proved to be more difficult than assessing their economic achievements. The application of Richardson's SIA scale proved to be extremely useful in this regard. By relating the migrants' opinions, judgements and economic achievements to their assessment of their satisfaction with aspects of Australian life, it was possible to show why some had become acculturated in a remarkably short period while others had never even become satisfied with Australia. A central aspect of their assimilation had been identified by Harold Holt, a former Minister for Immigration: 'The British newcomer,' he said, 'though he speaks the same language, has ties of kinship, tradition and history with Australians, and understands the general principles that form the basis of our great democracy, can also find himself lonely and misunderstood at times in the new country.' For, although Australia, especially in the late 1940s, had strong political and economic ties with Britain, its character was only superficially British. Australia had its own culture, forged by unique historical circumstances and processes.

The British migrant, though not disappointed with his higher wages, soon discovered that the children of this culture had explicit and often uncomplimentary views about his worth. The Appleyard survey showed that a migrant's experience in coming to terms with Australian society depended upon whom he had met and with whom he had personal contact. It also had much to do with his own personality. Richardson's analysis concluded that a British migrant's degree of satisfaction with Australian life depended on the progress he was making towards his current goals. These might be different from those goals he had expressed before emigrating; but what mattered most was whether or not he felt he was on the way to attaining them. A sense of being able to cope and a degree of social optimism were crucial to the achievement of satisfaction, which was generally reached when the migrant felt that his standard of living was at least no worse, and preferably better, than it had been before emigration.

In order to become identified with Australia, as defined by Richardson, a migrant needed to have developed a strong attachment to Australia. For his wife, the existence of parents who had approved of the move to Australia was very important. Furthermore, close mixing with Australian-born residents did much to make the migrant feel more Australian than British. Of great importance in reaching the final, acculturation stage of assimilation was the extent to which the migrant was involved in social activities. Achievement of acculturation depended upon how long the migrant had been in Australia, on whether he was a sociable person and on how often he had changed his residence and place of employment since arriving in Australia. Persons who reached the acculturation stage were more likely to have been active members of organisations, clubs and societies in Britain. Such persons were also self-reliant and predisposed to change.

Although the formal academic study identified important pathways

150

to assimilation, and separated the achievers from those who experienced difficulties, including many who returned to Britain, case studies reported in earlier chapters, and especially the experiences of the migrants interviewed by Granada researchers, placed the problems of readjustment that many faced in a much more humane and realistic light. Granada had interviewed three families and one single girl in England before they emigrated in 1965, and interviewed them again after they had been in Australia for about six months. Over 20 years later, in 1987, they were interviewed for a third time. Although each of the migrants so interviewed was clearly a satisfied settler, the experiences they related not only showed that they possessed those attitudes and traits that academics had concluded were necessary for successful settlement, but also provided details of the difficulties they had faced in Australia. The homesickness of the wife during her early days in Australia, together with the attitudes of some Australians, often combined to make life very unpleasant. It was on these occasions that the migrant's personality and determination to succeed proved to be crucial in reaching higher stages of assimilation.

During their fieldwork in 1987, Granada's researchers also interviewed a number of former assisted emigrants living in Britain as well as migrants still living in Australia. The information gathered on returnees clearly indicated how their ability to settle had been hampered by an inability to respond positively to good-natured banter about their British origins. It is quite clear, however, that some of their experiences were quite nasty; aggressive Australians seeing that some British migrants reacted negatively to 'Pom-baiting' were encouraged to increase their taunts.

Under the circumstances of the Assisted Passage Scheme, especially after the 1950s, rates of return by assisted migrants increased to about 15–20 per cent. These alarmed Australian officials not only because they represented a loss of money invested in outward passages, but also reflected poorly on Australia's economic and social situation and especially on the attitudes that some Australians had shown towards British migrants. Research conducted during the late 1950s indicated that about half the migrants who returned to Britain re-emigrated to Australia, some on second assisted passages. Although they had obtained significant increases in their incomes while in Australia, difficulties of adjusting to Australian society, especially the wife's homesickness, became so great that they decided to return. Many such

151

persons were Commonwealth nominees who had been accommodated in hostels from which they had never been able to move. Reaction to Britain on return was related to three main factors. The first factor was physical environment. Those who returned to the industrial cities had negative reactions. They had clearly forgotten that the environment had played an important part in their decision to emigrate in the first place. After the wide open spaces and relative cleanness of Australian cities and suburbs, many of them found it difficult to readjust to British city life. The second factor was family relations. Many returnees found that, while the home environment had not changed, *they* had. The experience of being in Australia, meeting new people and seeing new places had affected both their outlook and value patterns. Back in Britain, they saw home through new eyes, and the first excitement of meeting family and friends was often followed by a period of sobering readjustment. Those who had come back for a long holiday could stand aloof and muse on the situation, but those who had decided to return permanently were obliged to adjust to what was really a new and difficult situation. Their inability to take up personal relations where they had been broken off at emigration proved to be especially difficult for some returnees. Being intolerant of the way things were done in Britain did not assist their readjustment. The third factor was economic conditions: it was not easy to get used to working longer hours for the same or less pay on returning to Britain.

The Appleyard survey, conducted over a six-year period, confirmed that these aspects of return migration were important. When the researchers set out to reinterview the sampled migrants six years after they had arrived in Australia, they discovered that 29 per cent of the original group had returned to Britain, although about half had subsequently re-emigrated to Australia or moved to New Zealand. The return rates were 13–15 per cent for single men and women who married in Australia, 18 per cent for families, and 20 per cent for men and 37 per cent for women who remained single. These statistics were not surprising. Single emigrants who married Australian spouses would have more reasons to stay in Australia than single persons who perhaps had come originally to see Australia without any intention of remaining permanently. Married couples, on the other hand, were generally more committed to the venture. It was also more difficult for them to return to Britain, especially if they had large families.

Returnees in the Appleyard survey were divided into permanent

152

returnees and potential re-emigrants. Permanent returnees were more likely to have been motivated by failure to fulfil their material expectations of Australia than were potential re-emigrants. Also, the sense of being unsettled and insecure in Australia was much less apparent among returnees than among potential re-emigrants. Permanent returnees generally expressed great delight at being back in Britain, which they saw as 'everything Australia was not'. Many felt more secure and thought that their experiences in Australia had taught them to appreciate conditions and lifestyles in Britain. On the other hand, potential re-emigrants were far less satisfied with their situations. Many felt they had made a mistake in returning as soon as they reached Britain.

The net gains to Australia from post-war British assisted emigration have been very considerable. In demographic and economic terms the British contributions far exceed those of any other ethnic group. Until the early 1970s, Britons were accorded the highest priority as immigrants by Australian governments, even though the very generosity of the Assisted Passage Scheme attracted many persons who were destined to experience great difficulties of resettlement in what they thought, incorrectly as it transpired, would be a country and culture similar to their own. But the large majority of assisted migrants, whatever the nature of their preparation for Australia before departure, remained in Australia and applied their skills to the country's development, raised families, returned to Britain on visits and in due course became Australians in citizenship and outlook.

References

Appleyard, R.T., *British Emigration to Australia* (Weidenfeld and Nicolson, London and Australian National University Press, Canberra, 1964)

Appleyard, R.T., 'Determinants of Return Migration – A Socio-economic Study of United Kingdom Migrants who returned from Australia' (*The Economic Record*, September, 1962)

Barker, Dudley, *People for the Commonwealth* (Werner Laurie, London, n.d.)

Beijer G, Frijda N.H., Hofstede B.P. and Wentholt R., *Characteristics of Overseas Migrants* (The Hague, 1961)

Brown, L.B., 'English Migrants to New Zealand: A Pilot Rorschach Study' (*Australian Journal of Psychology*, Vol. 8, No. 2, 1956)

Calwell, Arthur A., 'Australia's Immigration Policy' (*The Australian Exporter*, July, 1948)

Crowley, F.K., 'The British Contribution to the Australian Population: 1860-1919' (*University Studies in History and Economics*, Vol. 11, No. 2, 1954)

Eisenstadt, S.N., *The Absorption of Immigrants* (London, 1954)

Isaac, Julius, *British post-war Migration* (Cambridge University Press, Cambridge, 1954)

Kiernan, Colm, *Calwell. A Personal and Political Biography* (Nelson, Melbourne, 1978)

Lucas, David, *The Welsh, Irish, Scots and English in Australia* (Australian Institute of Multicultural Affairs, Canberra, 1987)

Moore, Ronald E., *The Evolution of Australian Migration Policy:* the Transition from British Empire Preference to European Migration (1901-1952) (Master of Economics thesis, University of Western Australia, Nedlands, Western Australia)

Nadel, George, *Australia's Colonial Culture:* Ideas, Men and Institutions in mid-nineteenth century eastern Australia (Cheshire, Melbourne, 1957)

Nightingale, John, *Migrant Household Economic Behaviour* (Australian National University Press, Canberra, 1978)

Plant, G.F., *Overseas Settlement:* Migration from the United Kingdom to the Dominions (Oxford, 1951)

Richardson, Alan, *British Immigrants and Australia:* A Psycho-social Inquiry (Australian National University Press, Canberra, 1974)

Richardson, Alan, 'Some Psycho-social Aspects of British Emigration to Australia' (*British Journal of Psychology*, Vol. 10, 1959)

Walker, David, *We went to Australia* (Chapman and Hall, London, 1949)

Australia Day Statements by Arthur Calwell, January 21, 1947

Australia, Department of Immigration, *Digest,* Proceedings of Citizenship Conventions held in Canberra and papers presented by invited speakers, 1950 to 1970

Parliamentary Statements of Authur Calwell, August 2, 1945; March 5, 1946, November 22, 1946; November 28, 1947; September 8, 1949

Press Statements of Arthur Calwell, 1946 to 1949, held at Dept. of Immigration and Ethnic Affairs, Canberra

United Kingdom, *Final Report of the Royal Commission on the Natural Resources, Trade, and Legislation of Certain Portions of His Majesty's Dominions* (Dominions Royal Commission), Cd 8462, H.M.S.O, London, 1917

United Kingdom, *Papers of the Royal Commission on Population,* Report of the Economics Committee, Vol. 111, H.M.S.O, London 1950

Further Reading

Appleyard, R.T., *British Emigration to Australia*, (Weidenfeld and Nicolson, London, 1964)

Black, Peter, *The Poms in the Sun* (Joseph, London, 1965)

Brissenden, Alan, and Higham, Charles, *They Came to Australia* (Cheshire, Melbourne, 1961)

Carrington, C.E., *The British Overseas* (Cambridge University Press, 1950)

Cowley, Stewart, *The Whingeing Pom's Guide to Australia* (Colporteur Press, Sydney, 1985)

Donegan, Henry, *The Pommy Kid* (Publicity Press, Chippendale, 1970)

Jenkins, Thomas, *We Came to Australia* (Constable, London, 1969)

Jupp, James, *Arrivals and Departures* (Cheshire, Melbourne, 1966)

Kitson, Jill, *The British to the Antipodes* (Gentry, London, 1972)

Lewis, Roy, *Shall I Emigrate?* A Practical Guide (Phoenix, London, 1948)

Lort-Phillips, Patrick, *Pommies' Picnic* (Dymock's, Sydney, 1967)

Lucas, David, *The Welsh, Irish, Scots and English in Australia* (Australian Institute of Multicultural Affairs, Canberra, 1987)

Madden, A.F. and Morris-Jones, W.H., *Australia and Britain* Studies in a Changing Relationship (Cass, London, 1980)

Martin, J.I., *The Migrant Presence* (Allen and Unwin, Sydney, 1978)

Pepperall, R.A., *Emigrate to Australia* (Latimer, London, 1948)

Prentis, Malcolm, *The Scots in Australia* (Sydney University Press, Sydney, 1983)

Pringle, J.D. *Australian Accent* (Chatto and Windus, London, 1965)

Pryor, Oswald, *Australia's Little Cornwall* (Rigby, Adelaide, 1969)

Richardson, Alan, *British Immigrants and Australia* (Australian

National University Press, Canberra, 1974)

Sherington, Geoffrey, *Australia's Immigrants 1788-1978* (Allen and Unwin, Sydney, 1980)

White, Naomi and White, Peter, 'The 'British Disease' in Australia: press definitions and reality' (*Australian Journal of Communication*, Nos 1, 2, January, 1982)

MAP OF AUSTRALIA SHOWING STATES AND CAPITAL CITIES.

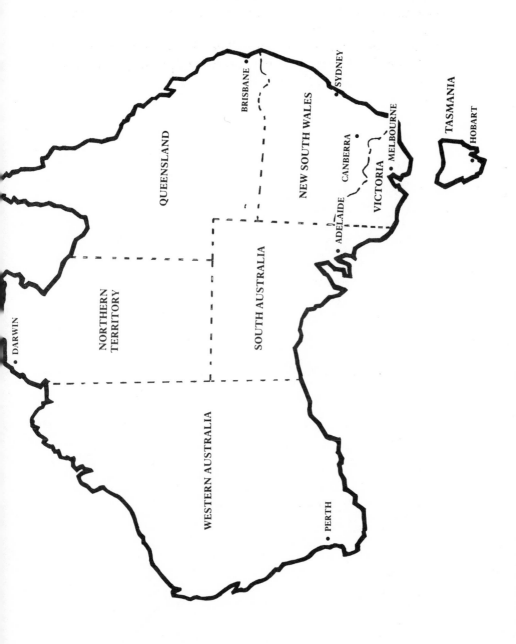

Settler Arrivals to Australia

YEAR	TOTAL SETTLERS	TOTAL U.K.	UNASSISTED U.K.	ASSISTED U.K.
1949/50	184889	52166	15134	37032
1950/51	153290	53341	14107	39234
1951/52	130462	59011	16057	42954
1952/53	95890	36757	12535	24222
1953/54	86468	26011	11282	14729
1954/55	124180	36281	11240	25041
1955/56	132628	37293	12061	25232
1956/57	120601	36024	12448	23576
1957/58	107978	41439	11470	29969
1958/59	116697	41623	13117	28506
1959/60	105887	38166	3829	34337
1960/61	108291	38004	2941	35063
1961/62	85808	30229	3051	27178
1962/63	101888	45750	3917	41833
1963/64	122318	60319	5440	54879
1964/65	140152	75956	5019	70937
1965/66	144055	75703	4645	71058
1966/67	138676	76502	5156	71346
1967/68	137525	62536	4765	57771
1968/69	175657	80684	4516	76168
1969/70 .	185099	77659	4802	72859
1970/71	170011	65535	4903	60632
1971/72	132719	55670	8329	47431
1972/73	107401	48681	13985	34696
1973/74	112712	46372	20243	26129
1974/75	89147	38313	18764	19549
1975/76	52748	17550	8071	9479
1976/77	70916	18714	10256	8458
1977/78	73171	21540	11847	9693
1978/79	67192	12767	9342	3425
1979/80	80748	16333	13639	2694
1980/81	110689	31512	25479	6033
1981/82	118031	38759	33313	5446
				1,137,587

Source: Department of Immigration and Ethnic Affairs, 'Australian Immigration' Consolidated Statistics, vols. 1 (1966), 8 (1976), 11 (1979), and 46 (1982).

Note: Before 1959, figures relate to permanent and long-term movement, and are not distinguished from settler movement.

160

SETTLER ARRIVALS TO AUSTRALIA

161

Index

experience 126
lifestyle 120
military forces 39
National Services 134
National University 98
outback 121–2
servicemen 55, 58
society 5, 59–60, 71, 79–80, 84,
114–15, 137, 141, 151
towns 118
traditions 95
Australia's Building Industry
Congress 97
colonial culture 83
commodity exports 6
history 84
Nationality and Citizenship Act
39
post-war development 14
post-war migration agreement 18

Baker, Noel 25
Barker, Dudley 25
Barnardo's home, Dr. 136
Bath 130
Beaumont, Michael 133–4
Belfast 131
Berlin airlift, the 147
Bevin, Ernest 25
Big Brother Movement 133
Bond, Alan 126
Borrie, W. D. 35–6, 39, 45, 97–8,
147
Boulder, Western Australia 118–120
BP Oil Refinery 113
Bradford, Yorkshire 137
Bring Out A Briton scheme 33–5,
38
Brisbane 132, 138
Britain, Australia's migration drive
in 31
birthrate in 7–8
decisions to leave 94
economic conditions in 38, 48,
96, 105, 109
family ties in 90

industrial cities of 101
inequality in 137
labour in 16
lifestyles in 153
nostalgia for 106
population in 10, 20
post-war 136
rationing and shortages in 2
reactions to life in 101
roots in 89
social structure and class system
in 58
wages in 106
British Commonwealth, future of 21
Commonwealth, interests of 38
emigration to Australia 51, 53, 55
migrants to Australia 24
National Health Service 81
Seamen's Union 113
system of social welfare 87
Broken Hill, New South Wales 129
Brown, L. B. 53–4
Bundaberg News Mail 20

Cabramatta Migrant Hostels 138
Calwell, Arthur 9–15, 17, 19–25, 27,
30, 36, 38, 83, 96, 144
Canada 6
Canberra 19, 146
Casey, Lord 25
census of 1986, The Australian 141
Chifley, Prime Minister Ben 11, 25,
27
Chitral 24
Churchill, Winston 7, 20–1, 145
Citizenship Act 42
Convention 27–8, 31–4, 35, 37,
42, 48–9, 69, 82, 97, 146–7
citizenship, Australian 153
class system, Britain's 148
Cleary, P.J. 34
climate, Australia's better 148
colonial office 5
Commonwealth populations,
redistribution of 25
convicts 5–6, 83

INDEX